Estates in Land and Future Interests
A Step-by-Step Guide

Estates in Land and Future Interests
A Step-by-Step Guide

Linda H. Edwards

Professor of Law
Mercer University

ASPEN LAW & BUSINESS
A Division of Aspen Publishers, Inc.
New York   Gaithersburg

Permissions
Aspen Law & Business
1185 Avenue of the Americas
New York, NY 10036

Printed in the United States of America.

1 2 3 4 5 6 7 8 9 0

ISBN: 0-7355-2441-6

Library of Congress Cataloging-in-Publication Data

Edwards, Linda Holderman, 1948-
  Estates in land and future interests : a step-by-step guide / Linda Holdeman Edwards.
    p. cm.
  Includes index.
  ISBN 0-7355-2441-6
  1. Estates (Law)–United States.   2. Future interests–United States.   I. Title.

KF577.E39 2002
346.7304'2–dc21

2001053940

About Aspen Law & Business
Legal Education Division

With a dedication to preserving and strengthening the long-standing tradition of publishing excellence in legal education, Aspen Law & Business continues to provide the highest quality teaching and learning resources for today's law school community. Careful development, meticulous editing, and an unmatched responsiveness to the evolving needs of today's discerning educators combine in the creation of our outstanding casebooks, coursebooks, textbooks, and study aids.

ASPEN LAW & BUSINESS
A Division of Aspen Publishers, Inc.
A Wolters Kluwer Company
www.aspenpublishers.com

For My Father
Lawrence Vincent Holdeman
1909–1994

Summary of Contents

Preface   *xvii*
Acknowledgments   *xix*

1. Introduction to the Study of Estates and
    Future Interests   1
2. Possessory Estates   7
3. Limitations Added to Possessory Estates   21
4. Future Interests Retained by the Grantor   39
5. Estates Followed by Remainders   51
6. Estates Followed by Executory Interests   71
7. Accounting for Additional Future Interests, Class
    Gifts, and Subsequent Divesting   83
8. Shifting and Springing Executory Interests   95
9. Review of Future Interests in a Second Grantee
    and the Estates They Follow   101
10. What Is the State of the Title?   107
11. Post-Conveyance Factual Developments   111
12. More Efforts to Further Alienability   127
13. The Infamous Rule Against Perpetuities   135
14. Applying the Rule Against Perpetuities   149
15. Relief from the Rule Against Perpetuities   165
16. Putting It All Together   169

Appendix A: An Alternative Outline of Estates and
               Future Interests   175
Appendix B: Vocabulary   179
Appendix C: Answers to Study Questions and
               Practice Exercises   185
Appendix D: Practice Exercises for Use in Class   219
Appendix E: Collection of Outlines and
               Summary Boxes   225

Index   *237*

Contents

Preface   *xvii*
Acknowledgments   *xix*

▶1: Introduction to the Study of Estates and Future Interests

Study Questions   *4*

▶2: Possessory Estates

The Nature of the Possessory Estate   8
The Fee Simple   9
The Fee Tail   10
The Life Estate   12
The Term of Years   13
What Can the Owner of a Fee Simple, a Fee Tail, a Life Estate,
or a Term of Years Convey?   14
What If the Conveyance Has No Words of Limitation?   16
What Happens to the Land When an Inherently Limited
Estate Ends?   16
Study Questions and Practice Exercises   *17*

▶3: Limitations Added to Possessory Estates

No Added Limitations   21
Added Limitations   23
    Recognizing the End of One Estate and the Beginning
    of Another   24
    The Determinable Estate   25
    Estates Subject to a Condition Subsequent   27
Non-Fee Simple Estates with Added Limitations   33

Two Reminders About Using the Chart 33
Memory Work 34
Study Questions and Practice Exercises 34

▶ 4: Future Interests Retained by the Grantor

No Future Interest Follows a Fee Simple Absolute 39
The Grantor's Future Interest Following an Estate That
Ends Naturally (A Reversion) 41
The Grantor's Future Interest Following a Determinable Estate (A
Possibility of Reverter) 42
The Grantor's Future Interest Following an Estate Subject to
a Condition Subsequent (A Right of Entry) 44
Identifying the Durational Nature of the First Future Interest 46
Study Questions and Practice Exercises 48

▶ 5: Estates Followed by Remainders

Remainders 51
Vested and Contingent Remainders 55
Ascertained Person 57
Class Gifts 58
Review of the Requirement That the Holder Be Ascertained 58
Condition Precedent 59
Remainders That Are Contingent for More Than One Reason 61
Adding "Vested" and "Contingent" to the Chart 61
Reversions Following Contingent Remainders 62
Alternative Contingent Remainders 64
Memory Work 66
Study Questions and Practice Exercises 66

▶ 6: Estates Followed by Executory Interests

A Determinable Estate Followed by an Executory Interest 71
Estates Subject to an Executory Limitation 75
Two Future Interests Held by the Second Grantee 79
Study Questions and Practice Exercises 79

▶ 7: Accounting for Additional Future Interests, Class Gifts, and Subsequent Divesting

Additional Future Interests 83
Vested Remainders Subject to Divestment 89

Describing a Vested Remainder Subject to Divestment   91
Vested Remainders Subject to Open   92
Study Questions and Practice Exercises   *93*

▶8: Shifting and Springing Executory Interests

Review of Shifting Executory Interests   97
Springing Executory Interests   97
Study Questions and Practice Exercises   *100*

▶9: Review of Future Interests in a Second Grantee and the Estates They Follow

Remainders   101
Executory Interests   102
Vested Remainders Subject to Divestment   102
Examples   103
Study Questions and Practice Exercises   *104*

▶10:What Is the State of the Title?

Optional Practice   *109*

▶11: Post-Conveyance Factual Developments

Deaths   112
Removal of Contingencies   113
Subsequent Vesting of a Contingent Remainder   115
Conveyance of a Fee Tail   115
Subsequent Conveyance of a Reversion or a Remainder   116
Future Interests Moving into Possession   117
Merger   118
The Continuation of Conditions: Destruction of
Contingent Remainders   120
Study Questions and Practice Exercises   *122*

▶12: More Efforts to Further Alienability

The Rule in Shelley's Case   127
Shelley's Case and Merger   129
The Doctrine of Worthier Title   130
Worthier Title and Merger   132

Review   133
Study Questions and Practice Exercises   *134*

▶ 13: The Infamous Rule Against Perpetuities

Preparing to Study the Rule   135
   Vested Interests vs. Contingent Interests   135
   Closed Interests vs. Interests Subject to Open   136
   When a Will Is Effective   137
   The Fetus (Gestation) Rule   137
   Medical Advances in Treating Infertility   137
   The Fertile Octogenarian   137
   The Unborn Widow   138
The Rule's Purpose   138
The Rule's Meaning   141
   Calculating the Permitted Time Period   141
   Deciding How Long an Interest Might Remain Contingent   141
   Validating Life   143
   An Example of an Interest That Violates the Rule   143
A Step-by-Step Approach for Applying the Rule   144
Study Questions   *147*

▶ 14: Applying the Rule Against Perpetuities

Danger Signs   149
   Examples   150
Analyzing Various Kinds of Future Interests   155
Study Questions and Practice Exercises   *160*

▶ 15: Relief from the Rule Against Perpetuities

The Effect of the Destructibility of Contingent Remainders Doctrine 165
The Charitable Exemption   166
Statutory Modifications of the Rule Against Perpetuities   167
Study Questions and Practice Exercises   *168*

▶ 16: Putting It All Together

Study Questions and Practice Exercises   *172*

Appendix A: An Alternative Outline of Estates and
              Future Interests   175

Appendix B: Vocabulary   179
Appendix C: Answers to Study Questions and Practice Exercises   188
Appendix D: Practice Exercises for Use in Class   219
Appendix E: Collection of Outlines and Summary Boxes   225

Index   *237*

Preface

When I began teaching Property, my students and I had a lot in common. True, I had struggled through a few weeks of Estates and Future Interests during my own law school education, but my only memories of the experience were of how lost my classmates and I felt. True, I had practiced law for quite a while, but nothing in my litigation practice had involved multiple ownership interests in Property. There was only one answer to my teaching dilemma: my students and I were going to have to learn Estates and Future Interests together.

Well, learn it we did, and we even had fun doing it. This book grew out of our study. It aims to demystify Estates and Future Interests — a notoriously complex and difficult area of Property law. Here are the book's main characteristics:

Clear, simple language. The concepts are hard enough. The language explaining them should be as clear and accessible as possible. This book is written to clarify, not add to the confusion.

Step-by-step approach. The book starts with simple, basic, concepts and builds upon them one step at a time. At each stage, new concepts are integrated with old material, and practice exercises help you master the material of that chapter before moving on.

One central graphic. Part of the problem with learning future interests is the morass of terms. This book provides a central graphic that organizes those terms and shows you how to analyze any conveyance.

Sensitivity to different learning styles. The book gives visual learners the graphics they need, contextual learners the overviews they need, auditory learners the textual explanations they need, and tactile learners the manual activities they need. The text sets out the material in multiple formats so everyone can find a tool that works.

Parallels Dukeminier and Krier's *Property* casebook. This book is written to work with any Property casebook, but it is purposefully designed to match the coverage and approach of Dukeminier and Krier's casebook, *Property*. All of the Future Interests concepts covered in *Property* are explained here, and nothing unnecessary is added.

Plentiful study questions and practice exercises. Practice is the best way to learn Estates and Future Interests. Each chapter in this book provides practice exercises (with answers) for learning the new concepts and reviewing material from earlier chapters.

Other study aids. In addition to the central graphic, the book provides three other kinds of study tools for organizing and using the terms and concepts: the outlines in Appendices A and E and the lists of available choices for identifying a conveyance in Chapter 10. Also, a vocabulary appendix provides quick reference for clarifying a particular term. Another appendix provides answers for the study questions and practice exercises. At the end of the book, all of the text boxes, lists, and charts are gathered into one appendix to provide a quick review of the entire book.

For students, we hope this book will give you the lay of this ancient land, and help you feel at home in the strange world of Estates and Future Interests. *For teachers*, we hope this book will raise the level of understanding your students achieve outside of class, reducing the need for basic explanation and repetition and freeing you to use class time more productively and enjoyably.

So, relax and let's see what lies in store as we begin our study of Estates and Future Interests in land.

November 2001   Linda H. Edwards

Acknowledgments

I am grateful to many people for their invaluable assistance during the planning and writing of this book. My deepest thanks go to my family, Dan, Emilie, and Katie Edwards and Frances Holdeman, for their enduring patience and support. For invaluable encouragement and many important suggestions, I thank Susan Belson, Joe Claxton, Larry Dessem, Dan Edwards, Paul Lewis, Jim Parker, Terry Pollman, Lucia Sellechia, Helene Shapo, and the anonymous developmental reviewers whose comments were so helpful. I am especially indebted to Joel Cornwell and Jack Sammons for their willingness to read and re-read earlier drafts with such care. I count their friendship among my greatest blessings.

The Rule Against Perpetuities coverage is greatly enhanced by Professor Brainerd Currie's mystery story, and I am happy that his legacy lives on. Jane Burns and Barbara Blackburn provided wonderful production support, friendship, and humor in the trenches, and Peggy Rehberger and Sherry Goldbecker painstakingly redeemed the text from many errors. Once again Betsy Kenny of Aspen Publishing has given me the benefit of her masterful editorial assistance. Thank you, Betsy.

Finally, I acknowledge with pleasure my 1996–2001 Property classes and thank them for teaching me estates and future interest. I hope I have done them justice.

Introduction to the Study of Estates and Future Interests

1

Nearly a thosand years ago, in 1066, William of Normandy crossed the English Channel, won the Battle of Hastings, and took possession of much of what is now England. In the years that followed, the Norman conquerors developed the beginning of today's system of land ownership: the system of possessory estates and future interests in land.

That system, with some modifications here and there, has been in place for nearly a millennium and the story of its creation and evolution is one of the most fascinating historical studies in Western civilization. Understanding the historical development of the concepts we'll be studying can be quite helpful. Many of the terms and concepts you will learn in this book will make much more sense to you if you also study the story of their development. Without a sense of how and why the various interests developed, you may find yourself puzzling over why we have so many names for such similar interests in land and why these minute distinctions really mattered.

Ideally, you will be studying the history of these estates and future interests simultaneously with your work in this book. The history will tell you why some of the terms and doctrines developed. The role of *this* book is to help you put that mass of information into a cohesive framework so you can analyze a conveyance and answer this dreaded question: What is the state of the title?

This book is a basic introduction. It does not cover all of the rules and doctrines that may implicate estates and future interests law. It does not attempt to say everything that could be said about the rules and doctrines it does cover. If it were to do those things, it would lose its ability to introduce you to a number of complicated concepts as simply as possible. If you continue your study of estates and future interests, you will find that the cases and materials sometimes use different terminology and sometimes disagree on relatively minor points. These differences are not important to your initial introduction to the area. There will be time enough for pondering these finer points after you have a general picture of the landscape.

We will study the system of land ownership by studying the conveyances that create interests in land. Our material will build in complexity rapidly, so it is best to start simply. Consider the simplest example:

O to A.

"O" stands for the owner. Another way to refer to O is as the ***grantor***, the person who is conveying (granting) an interest in the land to someone else. Unless otherwise indicated, we'll assume that O is the sole owner of all possible interests in the land. "A" stands for the person to whom O is conveying. Another way to refer to A is as the ***grantee***, the person receiving the grant from O. As we progress in the study of the estate system, we'll add more grantees. We'll eventually meet "B" and "C" and occasionally even "D." When we deal with the estate of a person who died with a will (a "testator"), we'll sometimes call that person "T."

These letter-names will also include reference to the person's successors in interest. A person's successors in interest include anyone to whom that person has given or sold the interest. For instance, if O owns a tract of land and dies, willing the land to her son, then O's son is O's successor in interest.

Before we begin, here are some hints for your study of possessory estates and future interests:

1. The study of possessory estates and future interests is mostly the study of a set of terms. If you approach the subject as primarily the study of a new set of vocabulary words, you'll be off to a great start. Every time a key term is introduced, the term will appear in bolded italics. When you see such terms, make a special note. Practice using those terms, and be sure you know them before you go on to the next chapter. Doing the Study Questions and Practice Exercises and making the flash cards will be a big help. If you forget a term, consult the vocabulary list in Appendix B.

2. You'll soon see how important it will be to read and digest every word and punctuation mark of a conveyance. As a matter of fact, one of the most significant benefits of the study of estates and future interests is the development of this skill of careful, precise reading— a key lawyering skill. The nature of a client's property interests can change completely depending on one word. Read each conveyance in the same way you would read an algebraic equation. Every word and punctuation mark matters.

3. Master the material as you go along. Try to learn all of the concepts in each chapter before moving on to the next one. Since each

chapter builds on the prior chapters, you'll need to study the material as you encounter it, rather than simply reading it and planning to come back to study it later. Even if you study a chapter thoroughly on the day it is assigned, you'll find that when you wake up the next morning, you will have forgotten much of it. This is normal. The best thing to do is to practice with the flash cards for half an hour each day. That way you'll be able to start moving some of this new information from short-term memory into longer-term memory, and you'll be able to integrate new material into prior material.

4. Learn to use the flowchart we'll be creating. The chart will show you how all of these new terms and concepts relate to each other. If you can understand and use the chart, you will understand the material. Especially if you are a visual learner, the chart will help you organize and learn the material. Whether or not you are a visual learner, the chart will guide you in analyzing any conveyance. If you simply work your way from left to right across the chart, the chart will prompt you to ask the right questions and to select the correct names for the various interests.

5. Appendix E contains an outline version of the chart, setting out the various categorizations of estates and future interests. It also contains, gathered into one place, copies of all of the summary boxes that appear in the text. Toward the end of your study, this appendix will provide an easy way to review key points.

6. Appendix A provides an alternative to the chart—an outline approach to finding the correct names for the various estates and future interests. Once we have covered most of the terms, you may want to refer to this outline as well. The goal is to use the approach (the graphic chart, the outline version of the chart in Appendix E, or the alternative to the chart in Appendix A) that works best for your own learning style.

7. Review the Study Questions, do the Practice Exercises, and practice with the flash cards. Even the act of preparing the flash cards is a study technique that will help you learn the material from that chapter. The complexity of the material will build quickly. Do not expect to be able to understand and retain all of this information without daily practice.

8. Approach the subject as if you are learning the rules of a new game. If you relax and work at it, the study of possessory estates and future interests can actually be fun.

Here are a few of the terms you'll need to know before we begin. Pay particular attention to the italicized sentences. You'll need to remember them to avoid making mistakes in future chapters.

Decedent: A dead person.

Testate and Intestate: A decedent dies "testate" if he or she dies with a will. A decedent dies "intestate" if he or she dies without a will.

Heirs: "Heirs" are the people who inherit real property from a decedent who dies intestate (without a will). Heirs are identified by statute in each state. They usually include the person's spouse and children. If no spouse or children have survived the decedent, heirs may also include grandchildren, parents, siblings, or other relatives. *Because heirs are determined at the time of death, living people have no heirs— only heirs apparent.*

Devise and Devisees: To "devise" is to pass real property by will. ("Martin Crowe devised his property to his stepson.") The person receiving the property is a "devisee." Notice that the words "heirs" and "devisees" do not mean the same thing. Devisees are beneficiaries under a will. Heirs inherit property *not* disposed of by a will. *A will does not create any interest in property until the testator dies.*

Bequest and Bequeath: To "bequeath" is to pass personal property by will. A decedent who dies testate "bequeaths" his or her personal property to those named in the will. The property itself is called a "bequest."

Issue: A person's lineal descendants all the way *down* the line. Issue include children, grandchildren, and all other **lineal descendants** to the point where the biological line dies out.

Ancestors: A person's biological forebears all the way *up* the line. Ancestors include parents, grandparents, great-grandparents, and all other lineal forebears.

Collaterals: All blood relatives other than issue or ancestors. Collaterals include siblings, cousins, aunts, uncles, nieces, and nephews.

Escheat: If a decedent has no heirs or devisees, the interest in land "escheats" (passes) to the state.

Convey: A person "conveys" land when that person transfers it to someone else. The land can be conveyed by sale or by gift. In either case, the transaction is a "conveyance."

▶ Study Questions

Learn the material in this chapter before you go on to the next chapter. Purchase a package of index cards and begin making your own set of flash cards to study. Begin with the following questions, the answers for which appear in Appendix C. In each succeeding chapter, make additional flash cards out of the Study Questions and Practice Exercises. *Include the number of the exercise so you can identify the question later.* Add them to the cards you have already made, shuffle, and practice with them all again.

1-1 What is the term for relatives like aunts, uncles, cousins, brothers, and sisters?

1-2 What is a "devisee"?

1-3 Is there something wrong with the following sentence? If so, correct it.

> *All of the heirs gathered at the lawyer's office to learn what the decedent had left them in his will.*

1-4 Fill in the blank: Anne Smith has made an appointment with her lawyer to have her will drawn. She intends to _____ her house to her son.

1-5 Fill in the blank: Jeremy Parker died _____ [without a will].

1-6 Are "convey" and "sell" synonyms? If not, why not?

1-7 Fill in the blank: The _____ [dead person] had no heirs.

1-8 Name some examples of a person's "collaterals."

1-9 Is there something wrong with the following sentence? If so, correct it.

> *Since Harold did not have a will,*
> *Maude is the devisee of his entire estate.*

1-10 What is the term for a person's children and grandchildren?

1-11 What is the term for a person's parents, grandparents, and great-grandparents?

1-12 Fill in the blank: Hazel's will left a _____ [an item of personal property disposed of by a will] to her brother.

1-13 Fill in the blank: If Hazel had not died _____ [with a will], all of her estate would have passed to her daughter.

1-14 Name some examples of a person's "issue."

1-15 Francine had never married. She died without a will, and all of her blood relatives had died many years before. Therefore, her property will _____ to the state.

1-16 Is there something wrong with the following sentence? If so, what?

All of Barbara's heirs are coming to visit her this summer.

1-17 David's father has just written a will naming David as the sole beneficiary of the family business. What property interest does David have as a result of being named in the will?

Possessory Estates

2

Perhaps the most distinctive characteristic of the English system of land ownership is its ability to recognize multiple "owners" of land. The English estates system recognizes that someone may own the right to possess the land now, while someone else may own the right to possess that same land at some point in the future. The owner of the right to possess the land now, in the present, owns the ***possessory estate***. The owner of the right to possess the land in the future owns a ***future interest*** in the land. Thus, the subjects of our study are "possessory estates" and "future interests."

Possessory Estate	Future Interest
→ → →	→ → →

As we study the system of land ownership, we will build a chart to organize the material. Our chart will be divided into sections, each referring to a separate interest. The first section will refer to the possessory estate (the right to possess the land now), and the next section will refer to the first future interest. And since it is possible to have more than one future interest, later we'll add another section to refer to a second future interest. If we had room, we'd add several more. Here is the beginning of the chart:

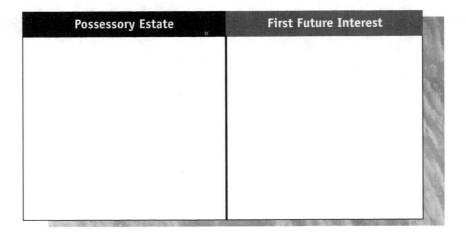

The next step in building the chart is to learn some additional information about the possessory estate. We will study two kinds of information about the possessory estate, the "nature" of the estate and any "added limitation." Therefore, we'll divide the "Possessory Estate" column in half, creating columns for "Nature" and "Added Limitation." We'll number the columns for easy reference, like this:

Possessory Estate		First Future Interest
❶ Nature	❷ Added Limitation	

▶ The Nature of the Possessory Estate

Recall that the estate system is able to divide land ownership into time periods. In keeping with that key feature, the "nature" of the possessory estate primarily tells us the *duration* of that estate. Here are the four possessory estates we will study:

the fee simple

the fee tail

the life estate

the term of years

The key distinction among these estates is how long they might last.

▶ The Fee Simple

The *fee simple* is the largest of these estates. A fee simple has no *inherent* ending—that is, no ending that is built into the estate by its very "nature." The owner of a fee simple can keep the land forever, can sell it or give it to someone else who can keep it forever, or can bequeath it to someone who can keep it forever. If the owner dies intestate, the owner's heirs will inherit the land. Any of these future owners of the fee simple estate can sell or bequeath the land, just as the original owner could. Most real estate transactions involve the sale of a fee simple estate in land. If you have bought a home, you probably have bought a fee simple estate in that land.

The classic language for creating a fee simple is this:

O to A __and [his or her] heirs__.

If you see the words "and [his or her] heirs" in a conveyance, you will know that the estate being conveyed is a fee simple.[1]

The words "to A" are the ***"words of purchase."*** "Purchase" here refers not to a sale but simply to a conveyance, whether by sale or by gift. The words of purchase tell you *who* is receiving the interest; in other words, they identify the grantee. They do not tell you what *kind* of estate the grantee is receiving. The words "and [his or her] heirs" tell you what *kind* of *estate* the grantee is receiving. These are the ***words of limitation*** because they tell you what kind of limitation (if any) is inherent in the estate. Remember that the key distinction among the four possessory estates is whether and to what degree they are *inherently* limited in duration. The words of limitation tell you whether the estate will end naturally and, if so, when. A fee simple will *not* end naturally.

---

[1] The words "and [his or her] heirs" express the historically defining characteristic of a fee simple: The grantee's heirs can inherent the right to possession.

O to A and her heirs.

Words of purchase   Words of limitation

In the case of the fee simple, the words of purchase ("to A") tell you that A is the grantee. The words of limitation ("and her heirs") tell you that A is receiving a fee simple rather than one of the other three possessory estates. Therefore, you know some things that A can do. You know that A can sell, give away, or bequeath the land. You know that if A dies without a will, A's heirs can inherit the land. You know all this simply by noticing the words of limitation ("and her heirs") in the conveyance.

It is important to remember that the words "and [his or her] heirs" do *not* convey any legally recognizable interest to A's heirs.[2] These words mean *only* that A is receiving a fee simple, an estate capable of being passed by inheritance. However, the conveyance does not create any rights in the persons who may or may not eventually be A's heirs. Until you get used to the terminology of the estate system, you will find yourself tempted to think that the conveyance "O to A and her heirs" conveys an interest to A *and* to A's heirs. So when you see the words "and [his or her] heirs" in a conveyance, mentally translate those words as "in fee simple." A has a fee simple, and A's heirs have nothing. You might even want to draw a line through the words "and [his or her] heirs" so those words don't confuse you.

Look ahead to page 14 for our next version of the chart. Notice that the words "Fee Simple" are placed in column 1 along with the words "no inherent end" to remind you of the distinctive characteristic of a fee simple. Also, the chart includes the words of limitation "and his/her heirs" to remind you of the words that identify a fee simple.

▶ The Fee Tail

Unlike the fee simple, the *fee tail* (in its original form) is subject to several important restrictions—restrictions that are inherent in its very "nature."[3] If O conveys an estate to A in fee tail, A possesses the land right now, but A cannot sell or give or bequeath the right to possession after A's death. Instead, when A dies, the land passes automatically to A's issue (A's next lineal descendants) regardless of whether A has a will. If A holds the land in a fee tail (in its original form), A can do nothing that would prevent the land from passing to his or her issue.

---

[2] Remember that A will not have any heirs until A dies. See page 4.

[3] In this initial description of the fee tail, we'll be referring to the original fee tail as it was first created. On page 15, we'll see that statutes in many jurisdictions now change some of the characteristics of the traditional fee tail. In order to understand these modern statutes, however, you'll first need to understand the original form of the fee tail.

Notice that land held in fee tail does not pass to A's issue by inheritance, even if A's issue are also A's heirs under the governing statute. Nor does the land pass to A's issue by bequest, even if A's issue are also the devisees under A's will. Instead, the land passes to A's issue because it is held in fee tail. Therefore, we do not say that A's issue "inherit" the fee tail or that they receive it "by bequest."

Lineal descendants can go on for a very long time, but the law presumes that at some point, the line will die out. Therefore, a fee tail is an *inherently* limited estate. The law presumes that at some point it will end naturally. We say that it will end naturally because it is in the very nature of a fee tail estate to end eventually. No one need do anything to make it end. It will end simply because it is a fee tail. We will soon see what happens after the fee tail ends. For now, however, just be aware that the estate ends when the last lineal descendant dies.

The classic language for creating a fee tail is this:

O to A *and the heirs of [his or her] body*.

Again, the words "to A" are **words of purchase**. They tell you who is receiving the interest. The words "and the heirs of [his or her] body" are the **words of limitation**. They tell you what kind of estate the grantee is receiving. In this case, they tell you that A is receiving a fee tail rather than one of the other three possessory estates. Therefore, you know some things that A can and cannot do. If A holds a fee tail (in its original form), you know that A cannot sell, give away, or bequeath the right to possess the land after A's death. You know this simply by noticing the words of limitation ("and the heirs of [his or her] body") in the conveyance.

O *to A* *and the heirs of her body*.
Words of purchase Words of limitation

As we saw with the fee simple, you'll need to remember that the words "and the heirs of her body" do *not* convey any legally recognizable interest to A's heirs or issue. These words mean *only* that A is receiving a fee tail. Until you get used to the terminology of the estate system, you will find yourself tempted to think that the conveyance "O to A and the heirs of her body" conveys an interest to A *and* to A's heirs or issue. So when you see the words "and the heirs of her body" in a conveyance, mentally translate those words as "in fee tail." As with the conveyance of a fee simple, you might want to draw a line through the words "and the heirs of her body" so those words don't confuse you.

Look at the chart on page 14. Notice that the words "Fee Tail" are placed in column 1. The words "passes to issue until line runs out" will remind you of the distinctive characteristic of the fee tail. The chart also includes the words of limitation that will help you identify a fee tail: "and the heirs of his/her body."

▶ The Life Estate

The *life estate* is inherently even more limited in duration than the fee tail. Like the fee tail owner, the owner of a life estate has only the right to possess the property in his or her lifetime. The owner of a life estate (the "life tenant") cannot sell, give, or bequeath the right to possess the land after the owner of the life estate dies. However, unlike the fee tail, a life estate does not pass to the owner's issue (lineal descendants) on death. Instead, the life estate simply ends. What happens then, you might wonder? We shall soon see. For now, however, just be aware that a life estate ends when its holder dies.[4]

The classic language for creating a life estate is this:

O to A *for life*.

Again, the words "to A" are the *words of purchase*, and they identify the grantee. The words "for life" are the *words of limitation*, telling you what kind of estate the grantee is receiving. They tell you that A is receiving a life estate rather than one of the other three possessory estates. Therefore, you know some things that A can and cannot do. You know that A cannot sell, give, or bequeath the right to possess the land after A dies. You know that A's heirs cannot inherit the land and A's devisees cannot take the land by bequest. You know all this simply by noticing the words of limitation ("for life") in the conveyance.

O *to A for life*.
Words of purchase   Words of limitation

Look at the chart on page 14. Notice that the words "Life Estate" are placed in column 1. The words "ends when holder dies" will remind you of the distinctive characteristic of the life estate. The chart also includes the words of limitation that will help you identify this conveyance: "for life."

---

[4] A life estate can be measured by the life of someone other than its holder. In that case, the life estate ends upon the death of the measuring life. See page 15. Unless otherwise noted, we will assume that the life estates in the examples in this book are measured by the life of the holder.

▶ The Term of Years

The **term of years** is the last of the four possessory estates. A term of years is commonly known as a lease.[5] The term of years has less status than the other three estates. The other three possessory estates are called "freehold estates," the owners of which are said to have **seisin** (the right to possession of land accompanied by particular responsibilities such as the payment of taxes). The term of years is a non-freehold estate. It arises when an owner of one of the other varieties of estates (a fee simple, fee tail, or life estate) promises to let someone else use the land for a set period of time. When that time is up, the lessor's right to use the land ends. The leaseholder cannot sell, give, or bequeath the right to use the land beyond the lease period. The leaseholder can use the land only during the period of the lease. Like the fee tail and the life estate, the term of years is inherently limited. It will end naturally, simply because it is a term of years.

The classic language for creating a term of years is this:

> **O to A _for 10 years_ [or for some other identified period of time].**

Again, the words "to A" are the **words of purchase**, and they identify the grantee. The words "for 10 years" are the **words of limitation**, telling you what kind of estate the grantee is receiving: a term of years. Therefore, you know that A cannot sell, give, or bequeath the right to use the land beyond the lease period. You know this simply by noticing the words of limitation ("for 10 years") in the conveyance.

> **O _to A_ _for 10 years_.**
> Words of purchase   Words of limitation

Now examine the chart on page 14 again. Notice that the words "Term of Years" are placed in column 1. The word "lease" will remind you of the meaning of a term of years. The chart also includes an example of the words of limitation that identify a lease: "for 10 years."

Notice also that the new material on the chart is shaded. Throughout this book, new material will be shaded the first time it appears on the chart so you can find it quickly. As the chart becomes more complex, the shading will help you orient yourself visually.

---

[5] There are several kinds of leases other than a term of years, but it is common to use the name "term of years" to refer generally to a leasehold estate.

Possessory Estate		First Future Interest
❶ Nature	❷ Added Limitation	
Fee Simple • *no inherent end* • *"and his/her heirs"*		
Fee Tail • *passes to issue until line runs out* • *"and the heirs of his/her body"*		
Life Estate • *ends when holder dies* • *"for life"*		
Term of Years • *lease* • *"for 10 years"*		

▶ What Can the Owner of a Fee Simple, a Fee Tail, a Life Estate, or a Term of Years Convey?

The owner of an estate can convey part or all of what the owner has[6] but not more. Therefore, the owner of a fee simple can convey all of that interest (by conveying a fee simple) or only part of that interest (by conveying a lesser estate such as a life estate or a term of years).

Simple enough. Now, what about the owner of a lesser estate? What can he or she convey? Consider the following conveyance:

O to A for life.

We know that A has a life estate. What, if anything, can A convey?

Start with the basic proposition we just learned: The owner of an estate can convey part or all of what the owner has but not more. Therefore, as we learned on pages 10-12, the holder of a life estate or a fee tail (in its original form) cannot convey an interest extending

---

[6] The ability to convey can be limited either by statute or by contract. For instance, some leases provide that the leasehold cannot be conveyed. We say that such a lease is not "assignable."

beyond the holder's life. In the case of a fee tail, we already know that upon the holder's death the interest in the land will automatically go to the holder's next lineal descendants. In the case of a life estate (our example above), we know that upon A's death, the life estate simply ends. There is nothing left of the interest after A dies—nothing left to convey.[7]

However, the owner of the estate *can* convey part or all of what the owner has. In the case of our example above ("O to A for life"), A has a life estate. This means that A has the right to possess the property for her lifetime. That is exactly what A can convey: the right to possess the property *for A's lifetime*. If A conveys her life estate to B, B has a life estate **pur autre vie** (pronounced "per o'tra vee"). The literal translation of the term "pur autre vie" is "for the life of another." B's life estate will be measured by the life of A. When A dies, B's interest in the land ends. And notice this: If B dies before A dies, B has died owning an interest in property, an interest that will continue until A dies. Therefore, B's heirs can inherit the life estate pur autre vie, or it can pass by will to B's devisees. Then, when A dies, the interest of B's heirs or devisees will automatically end.[8]

The owner of an interest in land can convey a lesser estate as well. For instance, imagine that A, the owner of a life estate, conveys to B a term of years for 10 years. What, if anything, does B have? B has a term of years for 10 years, but that term will end immediately upon A's death, even if the 10-year lease period has not expired. This is so because A cannot convey more than A has, and A has only a life estate.

What about the holder of a fee tail (in its original form[9])? Consider this conveyance:

O to A and the heirs of her body.

A has a fee tail, so A has the right to possess the land during A's life. A can convey what A has. If A conveys to B, then B has the right to possess the land *during A's life*. Immediately upon A's death, the right to possess the land passes to A's lineal descendants. If B should die before A dies, B's interest (the right to possess the land during A's life) can pass to B's heirs or devisees. But the moment A dies, the possessory estate passes to A's lineal descendants.

---

[7] As we shall shortly see, the right of possession will move back to O (A's grantor) or to another grantee specified in the original conveyance.

[8] The original grantor can create a life estate pur autre vie as well, like so: "O to A for the life of B."

[9] In Chapter 9, we shall see that modern statutes may alter the result of conveying a fee tail. In most states, a conveyance by the holder of a fee tail actually conveys a fee simple. For now, however, we will work with the original version of a fee tail because it better helps you understand the basic conceptual underpinnings of estates and future interests.

What if the holder of a fee tail (A) conveys a life estate to B? The principles are the same. B has the right to possess the land for B's lifetime, but only if A is still living. As soon as A dies, B's life estate ends, and the possessory estate passes to A's issue.

▶ What If the Conveyance Has No Words of Limitation?

Often you will see a conveyance with words of purchase but no express words of limitation. For example:

O to A.

How will you tell what variety of estate is intended? The modern rule is this: A grantor who does not use words of limitation is presumed to intend to convey all that the grantor could convey. If O had a fee simple, modern law presumes that O intended to grant a fee simple. So, under modern law, a fee simple can be conveyed either by the words "O to A *and [his or her] heirs*" or by the language "O to A."

▶ What Happens to the Land When an Inherently Limited Estate Ends?

So far we've been working with a simple conveyance to just one grantee. The conveyances we've seen are

O to A <u>and [his or her] heirs</u>. (Fee simple)

O to A <u>and the heirs of [his or her] body</u>. (Fee tail)

O to A <u>for life</u>. (Life estate)

O to A <u>for 10 years</u>. (Term of years)

We've seen that the last three of these estates have inherent limitations. They will end at some point. What happens then? The answer is this: *The grantor (or the grantor's successor) still has anything the grantor had and did not convey.* You can think of this concept like a pie. If the grantor (O) held a fee simple (the whole pie) and only conveyed a life estate to A (one slice), O still has all ownership interests except the life estate conveyed to A.

Who has the right to possess the land after A's life estate ends? O does because O didn't convey the right to possession after A's death. If O conveyed a fee tail, O has the right to possession when the fee tail ends. If O only conveyed a term of years, O has the right to possession when the term of years ends.

And what if O died before A's fee tail, life estate, or term of years ends? In this case, O died owning an interest in land (the interest left over after the conveyance of a lesser estate to A). That interest, the name of which we shall shortly learn, passes to O's heirs or devisees. Therefore, when A's lesser estate ends, O's heirs or devisees have the right to possession of the land.

▶ Study Questions and Practice Exercises

The chart provides a visual reminder of the four varieties of possessory estates. As you answer the questions, use the chart to remind yourself of these four varieties and what they mean. The answers appear in Appendix C. Do not go on to the next chapter until you have fully mastered the terms and concepts in this chapter. When you are ready to go to the next chapter, make questions 2-1 through 2-28 into flash cards *(including the number of the exercise so you can identify the question later)*, shuffle the cards together with the cards from Chapter 1, and review them all.

2-1 What is the name for the part of the conveyance that tells you *who* is receiving the conveyed interest?

2-2 What is the name for the part of the conveyance that tells you *what kind* of interest that person is receiving?

In the following conveyances, underline the words of purchase *and circle the* words of limitation, *if any. Beside each conveyance, write the name of the estate being conveyed to A (fee simple, fee tail, life estate, or term of years).*

2-3 O to A and her heirs.

2-4 O to A for 2 years.

2-5 O to A and the heirs of his body.

2-6 O to A for life.

2-7 O to A for the life of B.

2-8 O to A. (Assume modern law.)

What is the duration *of B's estate (if any)?*

2-9 O conveys to A and her heirs. (B is A's only child.)

2-10 O conveys to A for life. Then A conveys to B.

2-11 O conveys to A and the heirs of his body. Then A conveys to B. (Assume original fee tail.)

2-12 O conveys to A for 10 years. Then A immediately conveys to B.

2-13 O conveys to A for life. Then A conveys to B for 2 years. One month later A dies.

2-14 O conveys to A and his heirs. Then A conveys to B for 2 years. One year later A dies.

2-15 O conveys to A for life. In 1993, A conveys to B for 2 years. A dies in 2001.

2-16 O conveys to A and the heirs of her body. Then A dies, bequeathing her entire estate to her husband, B. A has one child, C.

2-17 O conveys to A for life. Then A dies, bequeathing her entire estate to B.

For each person other than O mentioned in the following questions, state whether that person has an interest in the property:

2-18 O to A and the heirs of his body. A has two sons (B and C) and two grandchildren (D and E).

2-19 O to A and her heirs. A has a husband (B) and one child (C).

2-20 O to A for the life of B.

2-21 O to A. A has no husband and no children but has a living father and mother. (Assume modern law.)

2-22 O to A for life. Then A conveys to B. B dies intestate with one heir, C.

After each of the following conveyances, state what interest A has and whether someone other than A has an interest in the property. If so, who and why?

2-23 O to A for 2 years.

2-24 O to A and the heirs of his body.

2-25 O to A for life.

2-26 O to A and her heirs.

2-27 O to A for the life of B.

2-28 O to A. (Assume modern law.)

The material we are studying has real-world applications for clients today. Here are several questions designed to show you how. In each of the questions, a client has come to you for advice. Try to answer the client's question before you refer to the answer in Appendix C.

2-29 "I have a 30-year lease on property located at Interstate Exit 109, and my lease allows me to build a building on the property. I want to use the property for a gas station, and I was about to talk to an architect about drawing up plans to build it. But I've just discovered that the deed of my lessor (the man who leased me the property) says that he has something called a 'life estate' in the property. Should I be concerned?"

2-30 "I have been diagnosed with a terminal illness, and I want to arrange my financial affairs in preparation for my death. My husband and I live in my parents' house, which they devised to me when they died. I own the house in fee simple. I want to be sure that my husband, who is disabled, can live in that house for the rest of his life. Upon his death, I want the house to go to my son by my first marriage. How can I arrange that?"

2-31 "My husband devised to me a life estate in the house he owned at his death. He devised all of the rest of his property to his son by his first marriage. I have been living in the house for the 10 years since he died. However, I am beginning to have health problems, and I want to move to the town where my daughter and her family live. Yesterday I put a 'For Rent' sign in the front yard, and last night my husband's son by his first marriage, Bob, called me. He said that I can't rent the house. He said that if I move out, the house goes to him. But I need the rental income from the house because I'll have to rent an apartment in my daughter's town. Is Bob right?"

Limitations Added to Possessory Estates

3

As we have seen in our chart, column 1 (the "Nature" column) lists the four kinds of possessory estates. We turn now to the second column under "Possessory Estate." We've titled it "Added Limitation" and numbered it column 2.

We have seen that the defining characteristic in column 1 is the *inherent* duration of the estate. A grantor can convey any of these four estates from column 1 just as they are, without adding any *additional* durational limitations. However, a grantor also may decide to add other durational limitations in addition to any limitations already inherent in the estate. Such added limitations are created by the grantor in the process of conveying the interest.

▶ No Added Limitations

First, we'll consider the situation in which the grantor decides *not* to add any additional limitations to the estate. If the grantor conveys a fee simple and does not add any additional limitations to the estate, we say that the grantor has conveyed a fee simple ***absolute***. The word "absolute" tells us that the estate has no limitations at all—no limitations inherent in its very nature (because the estate is a fee simple) and no further limitations added by the grantor. Only a fee simple can be "absolute" because only a fee simple can have no limitations of either kind.

Since a fee simple absolute is a fee simple with no added limitations, you can recognize it by seeing the words of purchase and words of limitation for a fee simple *and nothing else*:

O to A and [his or her] heirs.

[Fee simple absolute]

Look below for our next version of the chart. In column 2, notice the word "Absolute" and the words "No limitation" to remind you of what "absolute" means. This entry on the chart reminds you that one of the possibilities under "Added Limitations" is the possibility of no added limitation at all.

To give the state of the title for the conveyance above, you would start in column 1. You would select the nature of the possessory estate: fee simple. Then, from column 2, you would select "Absolute," since there is no added limitation. Therefore, the state of the title is this: *A has a possessory estate in fee simple absolute.*

What if the grantor conveys one of the *inherently* limited estates (a fee tail, life estate, or term of years) and does not include any *additional* limitations to that estate? In that case, we simply say that the grantor has conveyed that particular estate. There is no term to indicate the absence of added limitations for a fee tail, life estate, or term of years. The name of the estate itself (fee tail, life estate, term of years) tells us that the estate has *inherent* limitations. The absence of any added descriptive word tells us that the estate has no *additional* limitations. Therefore, if O conveys "to A for life," you would say that A has a possessory estate in life estate.

In column 2, we'll add a place for estates that will end naturally (the fee tail, life estate, and term of years) with no *additional* limitations. Since there is no term to describe the absence of an added limitation, we'll simply use four x's. The x's will tell you that you do not need to add a word to the name of the estate to indicate the absence of *added* limitations. We'll add the words "Will end naturally" to remind you of what the x's mean. Now the chart looks like this:

Possessory Estate		First Future Interest
❶ Nature	❷ Added Limitation	
Fee Simple • no inherent end • "and his/her heirs"	*No limitation:* **Absolute** ――――――― *Will end naturally:* **xxxx**	
Fee Tail • passes to issue until line runs out • "and the heirs of his/her body"		
Life Estate • ends when holder dies • "for life"		
Term of Years • lease • "for 10 years"		

Remember that columns 1 and 2 are just lists of options. *Do not try to connect them across the vertical line that divides them.*

▶ Added Limitations

We've covered the situations in which a grantor conveys either a fee simple or an inherently limited estate and adds no additional limitations. Now we come to the situation where the grantor wants to add another limitation to an estate. Assume that the grantor wants to convey a fee simple but wants the land back if a particular event happens. For instance, imagine a grantor who wants the land back if the grantee (A) ever gets a divorce. In that case, the grantor could convey a fee simple but would add a limitation that would bring the land back to the grantor if A divorces. This *added* limitation would make the fee simple a ***defeasible estate***, that is, a "fee" that is capable of being "de-feased" (brought to an end) by the occurrence of a particular event.

Two kinds of limitations can accomplish the grantor's wish to reclaim the property upon the occurrence of a particular event: a ***determinable*** limitation and a limitation making the estate ***subject to a condition subsequent.***

The difference between these two is subtle, but it can be important. The reason is this: The *determinable* estate will end *automatically* upon the happening of the limiting event. The grantor won't have to do anything. However, an estate subject to a condition subsequent will not end automatically upon the happening of the limiting event. To terminate an estate with an estate subject to a condition subsequent, the grantor will have to take some action to reclaim the property.

You can see why the distinction could be important. If the described event occurs, we cannot know who owns the possessory estate at that moment unless we know whether the limitation was determinable or subject to condition subsequent. If A owned a fee simple *determinable* (which ends automatically upon the happening of the event) and if the limiting event occurs, O now owns the possessory estate, even if O does nothing. A's estate has ended. However, if A owned a fee simple *subject to a condition subsequent* (which doesn't end automatically), A still owns the possessory estate. A will keep the fee simple subject to condition subsequent until O acts to reclaim the land.

Distinguishing between these two limitations can be difficult. The next few pages will describe the characteristics of each. As you compare them, you will be looking primarily for two drafting hints: (1) which words the drafter has chosen to introduce the limitation and (2) whether the limitation is placed before or after the punctuation that marks the end of the description of A's estate. Before we begin our study of each of the limitations, it may be helpful to clarify how we locate the end of the words describing A's estate.

▶ Recognizing the End of One Estate and the Beginning of Another

Examine the words of the following conveyance:

O to A until A's youngest child reaches 25, then back to O.

What marks the end of the description of A's estate and the beginning of the next estate (O's estate)? If you guessed "the comma," you're right. Draw a vertical line between the number "25" and the word "then." All the words before this line describe A's estate. The words after this line describe O's estate. Notice that, grammatically, the limitation "until A's youngest child reaches 25" is placed within the description of A's estate.

Now examine the words of another conveyance:

O to A, but if A sells liquor on the property, then back to O.

What marks the end of the description of A's estate and the beginning of the next estate (O's estate)? This one is harder, isn't it? Here we have two commas. Which comma marks the boundary between the two estates? In future interest law, we say that the *first* of the two commas signals the end of one estate and the beginning of another. Draw a line between "A" and "but." All the words before this line describe A's estate. The words after this line describe O's estate. Notice that the limitation "if A sells liquor on the property" is placed within the description of O's estate, even though practically speaking it will operate to limit A's estate.

Look again at the first of these two examples:

O to A until A's youngest child reaches 25, then back to O.

Could we rephrase this conveyance to place the limitation in O's estate and still accomplish the grantor's intent? You bet. How about this:

O to A, but when A's youngest child reaches 25, then to O.

Where does the description of A's estate end and the description of O's estate begin? At the first comma. Draw a line between "A" and "but." All the words before this line describe A's estate. The words after this line, including the limitation about A's youngest child reaching 25, describe O's estate.

We'll look at one more example before we start our study of defeasible estates:

O to A so long as A does not sell liquor on the property, but if A sells liquor on the property, then to O.

Where does the description of A's estate end and the description of O's estate begin? Again, it's at the first comma. Draw a line between the first "property" and "but." All the words before this line describe A's estate. The words after this line describe O's estate.

But notice that the limitation about selling liquor on the property actually appears in the words describing both estates. As we shall see in the next two sections, the key question will be whether the limitation appears in the description of the estate that might be ended by the happening of the limitation (A's estate). The limitation might be restated in the description of O's estate, but that will not concern us. The key question will be whether the limitation appears in A's estate.

Now we're ready to study *determinable* estates and estates *subject to condition subsequent* and the differences between them.

▶ The Determinable Estate

As we saw above, the key conceptual difference between a determinable estate and an estate subject to condition subsequent is this: A *determinable* estate will end *automatically* upon the happening of the condition, while an estate subject to a condition subsequent will not.

This conceptual difference is the basis for one of the ways to distinguish the two kinds of limitations. A determinable estate ends automatically because the limitation is the durational marker of the estate from the very beginning. The way the conveyance reflects this characteristic is that, grammatically, the limitation is placed within *A's* estate. Its grammatical function within A's estate is to serve as the durational marker of the estate given to A. Here is an example of a determinable estate:

> ***O to A and her heirs <u>so long as A does not divorce</u>.***

Notice that the grantor conveyed the fee only for the period of time until the condition occurs. By placing the limitation grammatically in the description of A's estate, the grantor has used the limitation as the measuring post for describing the duration of the estate conveyed. Therefore, when the limiting event occurs, the estate ends automatically because *the only estate conveyed to A was the right to possession until A divorces*.

The language creating the *determinable* limitation carries connotations of this distinction. A determinable estate is created using words of temporal limitation, like these:

> *O to A and her heirs <u>until</u> A divorces, then to O.*

> *O to A and her heirs <u>so long as</u> A does not divorce, then to O.*

O to A and her heirs <u>while</u> A has not gotten a divorce, then to O.

O to A and her heirs <u>during</u> the time that A remains undivorced, then to O.

Notice also that the words of temporal limitation (the phrases beginning with "until," "so long as," "while," or "during") are placed grammatically within the words describing the estate conveyed to A. They come *before the comma* that marks the end of the words describing A's estate.

This practice of analyzing the conveyance by working within the punctuation setting off the different estates will be critical as we continue our study of estates and future interests. You will have to read carefully, analyzing the conveyances much as you would analyze an algebraic equation. In the examples above, the estate conveyed to A is described by the words before the first punctuation mark. Sometimes a period or a semicolon, rather than a comma, may mark the end of the description of A's estate. However, the concept is the same. Work within the words set off by punctuation marking the end of A's estate.

So we see that several characteristics will help us recognize a determinable estate:

1. The added limitation is described by using words of temporal limitation, such as *until*, *so long as*, *while*, or *during*;

2. These words of temporal limitation indicate that the duration of the estate being conveyed is actually measured by the added limitation; and

3. The limiting words are placed before the first punctuation mark, the punctuation mark signaling the end of the description of A's estate and the beginning of the description of O's estate.

While the first punctuation mark is usually a comma, other punctuation marks can serve this purpose as well. Here are examples of conveyances that create a fee simple determinable using punctuation other than a comma:

O to A and her heirs <u>until</u> B graduates from college; then to O.

(This conveyance uses a semicolon rather than a comma.)

O to A and her heirs <u>so long as</u> A remains married.

(This conveyance uses a period. Here O's estate is not articulated at all, but we know that O has retained whatever O did not convey. Therefore, we know that after A's estate ends, the possessory estate will be in O, even if the conveyance doesn't say so.)

O to A and her heirs <u>while</u> A or one of A's issue lives on the property. If there comes a time when neither A nor one of A's issue lives on the land, then to O.

(This conveyance uses a period to mark the end of the description of A's estate. Notice that the limitation is stated again in the words describing O's estate. For our purposes, this makes no difference. The key question is whether the limitation appears inside the description of A's estate. Here it does.)

The defining characteristic of all of these estates is that the limiting language is durational (until, while, so long as, during) and is contained grammatically within the description of A's estate. Therefore, A's estate is *determinable*. The limitation "determines" the duration of the estate conveyed.

▶ Estates Subject to a Condition Subsequent

As we have seen, in a determinable estate, the language describing A's estate indicates that A's estate is marked durationally by the limiting event *from the instant of the estate's creation*. Grammatically, this distinction is indicated by placing the limitation within the description of A's estate, like so:

O to A and her heirs <u>until A reaches 21</u>, then to O.

By contrast, if A's estate is limited by a *condition subsequent*, A's estate is *not* marked durationally as a part of the description of the estate granted. Rather, the language describes the estate to be conveyed to A ("to A and her heirs"). After the description of A's estate is completed, the grantor adds a limitation giving the grantor the right to cut A's estate short ("but when A reaches 21, then back to O"). Grammatically, the limitation is placed *in O's estate*, not A's. It is placed *after* the punctuation mark that signals the end of the description of A's estate.

Thus, in our example, the "but when" language indicates that the limitation is not a part of the estate actually granted to A. Rather, it is *a right allocated to the estate that comes next*. It gives that estate the right to "interrupt" A's estate if the designated event happens. Thus, we can see that A's estate does not end automatically. The holder of the next estate (O) will be able to decide whether to interrupt A and reclaim the land or whether to allow A's estate to continue. Until O acts, A retains the right to possession.

In an estate subject to a condition subsequent, the words that introduce the limitation are words of express condition. The following are examples of words of express condition (words that create an estate subject to a condition subsequent):

O to A and her heirs, <u>but if</u> A divorces, then back to O.

O to A, <u>provided that</u> A does not divorce and if A divorces, then to O.

O to A, <u>on condition that</u> A does not divorce, and if A divorces, then to O.

O to A and her heirs; <u>however,</u> if A divorces, then to O.

All of these conveyances place the first mention of the limitation *in the description of the next estate* (O's). The fact that the limitation is placed in the *following* estate is the reason we say that the estate is subject to a condition *subsequent*. Upon the occurrence of the event, O's estate could *interrupt* the normal duration of A's estate, if O so chooses. The normal duration of A's estate is defined by the words creating A's estate.

You can see that, in the examples above, the words creating A's estate contain no limitation on its duration. Double check this by drawing a vertical line to separate A's estate and O's estate in each of these conveyances, just as you learned to do on pages 24-25.

Separating the two conveyances by a comma or some other punctuation mark is a drafting convention that can help distinguish between these two kinds of limitations. You cannot rely completely on this convention, for you may find conveyances in which the drafter has strayed from the convention. For instance, you may see a conveyance similar to the third conveyance above but unpunctuated, like this:

O to A <u>on condition that</u> A does not divorce and if A divorces then to O.

In this example, you have no punctuation mark to guide you in separating the descriptions of the two estates. Still, the conveyance uses a term of express condition ("on condition that"), so you can be pretty sure that A's fee simple is subject to a condition subsequent rather than a determinable limitation.

In this book, we will observe the drafting convention of separating the two estates with a punctuation mark. This drafting convention will ease your introduction to the sometimes difficult distinction between determinable estates and estates subject to a condition subsequent. It will also help you get into the drafting habit of using the convention to clarify the kind of limitation your client intends.

Therefore, in this book, you can assume that for a *determinable* estate, the limitation will be first articulated before the punctuation setting off A's estate and will use words of *temporal limitation*. For an estate *subject to a condition subsequent*, the limitation will *not* be articulated before the punctuation setting off A's estate and will use words of *express condition*.

Remember that when a grantee (A) has an estate subject to a condition subsequent (like the examples above) and when the described event occurs, O has the *right* to terminate A's estate. However, if O does not enforce that right, A's estate continues uninterrupted. A's estate does *not* end automatically, as it would if it were a determinable estate. Here are two more examples of conveyances that create a fee simple subject to a condition subsequent:

> *O to A and her heirs, <u>provided that</u> A does not get a divorce.*

> *O to A and her heirs, <u>on condition that</u> A does not use the property for a bar.*

Notice again that the conveyance does not have to say that the interest that follows A's estate is in O. We know that the subsequent interest is in O because we know that O still has whatever O did not convey, and O conveyed only A's estate. Therefore, we know who will have the right to interrupt A's estate if and when the described event occurs: O.

DISTINGUISHING ADDED LIMITATIONS

Determinable Estate:

1. The limitation is phrased expressly as the measure of the duration of the estate, using words like *until, so long as, while,* and *during.*

2. The limitation is placed *before* the punctuation mark signaling the end of the description of A's estate

   (a drafting convention only).

Estate Subject to a Condition Subsequent:

1. The limitation is phrased like an afterthought or a condition that allows the grantor to cut short an estate previously granted. It uses words like *but if, provided that, on condition that,* and *however.*

2. The limitation is placed *after* the punctuation mark signaling the end of the description of A's estate

   (a drafting convention only).

SUGGESTION	Recognizing the difference between words of temporal (durational) limitation (until, so long as, while, during) and words of express condition (but if, provided that, on condition that, however) will be critical in distinguishing between a determinable estate and an estate subject to a condition subsequent. From time to time, you may encounter other words or phrases used to introduce limitations, but the examples in the prior sentence and in the chart above are the most frequent. In order to make your introduction to future interests a little easier, we will use only these terms in this book. Your study of future interests will be a great deal easier if you simply memorize them now, along with the kind of limitation each signals.

▶ **Key Operational Distinction.** Remember that the key *operational* distinction between the two limitations is what happens if the event occurs. The determinable estate ends automatically, but the estate subject to a condition subsequent simply reserves the grantor's *right* to end A's estate. In effect, a grant subject to a condition subsequent allows the grantor to postpone deciding whether to end A's estate upon the happening of the described event.

Determinable estate ends automatically.	**Estate subject to condition subsequent ends only if and when O enforces the right to retake possession.**

You may be wondering what practical difference the distinction could make, since in order to take actual physical possession, O would have to take some action, even if A's estate is determinable. O would at least come onto the property and perhaps move some belongings onto the property as well. One answer is that sometimes we need to know who has the possessory estate (and therefore the *right* to possession), no matter who may have *actual* possession. For one example, see Practice Exercise 3-33.

Another example can occur in an adverse possession situation.[10] For instance, if A has a determinable estate and the triggering event

---

[10] If you have not yet studied the doctrine of adverse possession, disregard this explanation of how that doctrine might interact with the kind of future interest the grantor owns.

occurs, the possessory estate immediately returns to O. Then, if O does nothing and A remains on the land, A may be considered an adverse possessor. After the required period of time has gone by, A may have adversely possessed the land from O. However, if A had an estate subject to a condition subsequent and O did nothing, A still has the possessory estate, and, therefore, A's retention of possession is not adverse to the "true owner." Until O acts to reclaim the land, A *is* the "true owner" and therefore cannot adversely possess against herself. As a result, the statutory period does *not* begin to run, and A's continued possession will *not* establish title to the land through adverse possession.[11]

If you think that the distinction between these two kinds of limitations should be clearer, you're right[12] Careful drafting can go a long way to clarify the estate the grantor intends to convey, but, unfortunately, you probably will encounter some unclear conveyances. However, for this introduction to estates, we will avoid these ambiguities by using only the language and punctuation described above.

Turning to the chart on page 32, we'll finish filling in column 2 (for now) by adding the determinable limitation and the condition subsequent limitation. Notice the added reminders that a determinable estate could end early *by its own durational terms* and that an estate subject to a condition subsequent could end early *by interruption of the next estate.* So far column 2 covers the following kinds of situations:

▶ A's estate has no limits at all ("Absolute");

▶ A's estate has an inherent end (because it is not a fee simple) but no additional limitations (xxxx);

▶ A's estate has an additional limitation that marks how long it will last ("Determinable"); and

▶ A's estate is subject to O's right to reclaim it in case a particular event occurs ("Subject to a condition subsequent").

Compare this list with column 2 of the chart so you can be sure you know how to find the term that covers each of these situations.

---

[11] In most jurisdictions, these matters are governed by statutes that dictate what would happen in such a situation.

[12] In some jurisdictions, statutes have clarified the situation by eliminating the distinction between a determinable estate and an estate subject to a condition subsequent.

Possessory Estate		First Future Interest
❶ Nature	**❷ Added Limitation**	
Fee Simple • *no inherent end* • *"and his/her heirs"*	No limitation: **Absolute**	
	——————————	
Fee Tail • *passes to issue until line runs out* • *"and the heirs of his/her body"*	Will end naturally: **xxxx**	
	May end early by its own terms: **determinable**	
Life Estate • *ends when holder dies* • *"for life"*	*May be interrupted by next estate:* **subject to a condition subsequent**	
Term of Years • *lease* • *"for 10 years"*		

Now we'll practice working with the chart we have built so far. Consider the following conveyance:

> ### O to A and her heirs so long as B remains single, then to O.

▶ First, draw a line to separate the descriptions of A's estate and O's estate. Your line should be between the word "single" and the word "then."

▶ Now, use the chart to identify A's estate. Start with column 1, the "Nature" of the possessory estate. Column 1 lists the four choices for the "Nature" of the estate, and it gives us some reminders about each. Which variety of estate is this? A fee simple? A fee tail? A life estate? A term of years?

  If you decided that this conveyance creates a fee simple in A, you're right. The words of purchase ("to A") tell us who will have the estate, and the words of limitation ("and her heirs") tell us the nature of the estate: a fee simple.

▶ Now, move to column 2. Look again at the conveyance to see if the grantor has placed any *additional* limitations on the estate, that is, limitations in addition on any already inherent in the nature of the estate. Which choice accurately describes this conveyance? Is this fee simple absolute? No, because we can see an added limitation ("so long as B remains single"). We know the right answer isn't the second choice (represented by four x's) because this is a fee simple, not one of the estates that will end naturally. Since the grantor has added a limitation, we know that this is either a fee simple determinable or a fee simple subject to a condition subsequent.

To tell the difference, notice the durational language "so long as." Also notice that grammatically the limitation is placed in the words describing A's estate (before the comma) rather than in O's estate (after the comma). This is the language of a *determinable* limitation. Therefore, you know that this conveyance creates a *fee simple determinable* in A.

▶ Non-Fee Simple Estates with Added Limitations

In all of the prior conveyances, the defeasible limitations were attached to *fee simple* estates. However, any other possessory estate (a fee tail, life estate, or term of years) can be subject to a defeasible limitation, too. For instance, a life estate can be determinable or subject to a condition subsequent. Here is an example:

O to A for life, but if A divorces, then to O.

▶ First, draw a line to separate the descriptions of A's estate and O's estate. Your line should be between the word "life" and the word "but."

▶ Now, use the chart to identify A's interest. Start with column 1. The words of purchase ("to A") tell us that the possessory estate is in A. The words of limitation ("for life") tell us that A's estate is a life estate. Therefore, in column 1, we select "Life Estate."

▶ Now we move to column 2. Will this estate end naturally? Yes, but notice that there is also an added limitation that might cause it to end even earlier. Therefore, we'll need to choose either "Determinable" or "Subject to a condition subsequent." Now, which is it? We notice that the limitation is placed *after* the comma, in the description of O's estate. Also, the words introducing the limitation are words of express condition ("but if"). The limitation is articulated as a condition that will allow O to interrupt A's estate. Therefore, the correct choice is "Subject to a condition subsequent." The complete description for A's estate is a *possessory estate in life estate subject to a condition subsequent.*

▶ Two Reminders About Using the Chart

1. Understanding how to use the chart (or its outlined version in Appendix E) is going to be important as we continue through the rest

of the book. Learn to use it now, while it is relatively simple, and practice using it in succeeding chapters, as each layer of complexity is added to it. At the end, you'll see that the chart will organize a daunting amount of information for you so you won't have to do it yourself or be lost amid a confusing morass of terms. If you do your best to master the use of the chart and you cannot, try using the outline in Appendix A.

2. The entries in columns 1 and 2 are merely lists of the possible options in their respective categories. These lists are not related to each other horizontally. ***Therefore, don't try to move horizontally from an entry in column 1 to an entry in column 2.*** Simply select the appropriate choice from the list in column 1, and then, from among all the column 2 options, select the appropriate choice.

▶ Memory Work

Memorize the terms that commonly indicate a fee simple determinable and those that commonly indicate a fee simple subject to a condition subsequent:

Fee simple determinable:

until, while, so long as, during

Fee simple subject to a condition subsequent:

but if, provided that, on condition that, however

▶ Study Questions and Practice Exercises

Practice working with the material in this chapter, and learn it well before you go on to the next chapter. Answer the following questions, using the chart to help you where appropriate. Except for 3-32 through 3-34, make the questions into flash cards (*including the number of the exercise so you can identify the question later*), add them to your other cards, shuffle, and practice them all again.

3-1 Which estate(s) can be said to be "absolute"?

3-2 What are the inherently limited estates?

3-3 What kinds of estates "end naturally"?

3-4 Which kind of estate ends automatically upon the happening of a limiting condition: a determinable estate or an estate subject to condition subsequent?

3-5 Which kind of estate does *not* end automatically upon the happening of a limiting condition: a determinable estate or an estate subject to condition subsequent?

3-6 Name four examples of words or phrases of "temporal limitation," that is, words or phrases that signal a determinable estate.

3-7 Name four examples of words or phrases of "express condition," that is, words or phrases that signal an estate subject to a condition subsequent.

3-8 As between a determinable estate and an estate subject to a condition subsequent, which allows the grantor to postpone the decision about whether to enforce the condition?

3-9 As between a determinable estate and an estate subject to a condition subsequent, which uses the condition as the *durational marker* defining the length of the estate granted?

3-10 In which estate does the occurrence of the condition *interrupt* the prior estate: a determinable estate or an estate subject to condition subsequent?

In the following conveyances, draw a vertical line marking the end of the words describing the possessory estate and the beginning of the words (if any) describing the future interest. Beneath each conveyance, write the complete name of A's possessory estate. Use the chart to help you.

3-11 O to A so long as A does not divorce B, then back to O.

3-12 O to A and her heirs so long as A does not divorce B, but if A divorces B, then back to O.

3-13 O to A and his heirs, but if A divorces B, then to O.

3-14 O to A, on the condition that A does not divorce B.

3-15 O to A and his heirs, provided that A does not divorce B, then to O.

3-16 O to A until A divorces B, then back to O.

3-17 O to A; however, if A divorces B, then to O.

3-18 O to A and her heirs while A refrains from divorcing B.

3-19 O to A and her heirs during the time that A refrains from divorcing B, then back to O.

3-20 O to A. (Assume modern law.)

3-21 O to A, provided that A never drills for oil on the property.

3-22 O to A and his heirs for so long as A cares for B on the premises.

3-23 O to A for life or until B graduates from medical school.

3-24 O to A and the heirs of his body.

3-25 O to A for life, on condition that A never sells alcohol on the property.

3-26 O to A from September 1, 2002, until August 31, 2008.

3-27 O to A for 30 years while A resides on the premises.

3-28 O to A for the life of B.

3-29 O to A and the heirs of her body so long as the land is farmed, but if the land ceases to be farmed, then back to O.

Who has the right to possession at the end of each of the following series of events? Explain your answer.

3-30 Conveyance: "O to A until A graduates from law school, then back to O." Two years later A graduates from law school. O makes no attempt to retake the property.

3-31 Conveyance: "O to A; however, if A graduates from law school, then back to O." Two years later A graduates from law school. O makes no attempt to retake the property.

In each of the following questions, a client has come to you for advice. Answer the client's question.

3-32 "I own a small house that I presently use as a rental unit. My daughter has just graduated from college, and I want to give it to her as her first home. However, she isn't married yet, and I haven't really approved of most of the men she has dated. I want to be able to take the house back if she should marry someone I think will induce her to squander her equity in the home. How can I do that?"

3-33 "I was chasing my dog, who had run onto a lot with a boarded-up church building on it. I fell into an open hole on the property and broke my spine. I have lots of medical bills, and since I haven't been able to work, I have no way to pay them. I went down to the courthouse to see who owns the property, and I found a deed that read 'Alicia Baker conveys to the First Congregational Church for so long as the property is used for church purposes.' As far as I can tell, the First Congregational Church has closed, and all its members have gone to other churches. I don't think the church has any assets anymore. Is there anyone other than the church who might be responsible for my injuries?

3-34 "I have taken a job working in Spain, and I expect to be living in Madrid for a long time, maybe for the rest of my life. I don't want to rent my U.S. house because I won't be in the country to take care of it. Frankly, I don't expect to ever need it again. I had planned to devise it to my niece, but one never knows what life has in store, and if I did need it again, I'd like to have access to it. Is there a way that I could give it to my niece now but get it back if I move back to the States and need it again?"

Future Interests Retained by the Grantor

4

We now turn our attention to the question of what happens if A's possessory estate ends. As we learned in the last chapter, the grantor retains any interest not conveyed to someone else. Therefore, we already know *who* owns the future interests that follow each of the limited possessory estates. The grantor owned the right to future possession before the conveyance (by owning a fee simple). Since the grantor did not convey the right to future possession to a grantee, the grantor *still* owns that right.[13] In this chapter, we'll learn what to call future interests retained by the grantor.

On the chart, we'll need three columns to describe a future interest. In the first of these, column 3, we'll list the names for each "Kind of Future Interest."

▶ No Future Interest Follows a Fee Simple Absolute

No future interest follows a possessory estate in fee simple absolute. This is so because a fee simple is the largest possible estate and because the term "absolute" tells us that the grantor has not added any limitation to that estate. Therefore, the grantor has not retained any interest in the land. Since the grantor conveyed away all interest in the land, no future interest remains. We'll represent this on the chart by putting "NONE" in

---

[13] A grantor can convey the possessory estate to one grantee and the future interest to another grantee. We will study future interests conveyed to a second grantee in Chapter 5.

the column. If you get to this "NONE," in column 3, you'll know you are done identifying the state of the title.

Possessory Estate		First Future Interest		
❶ Nature	❷ Added Limitation	❸ Kind of Future Interest		
Fee Simple • *no inherent end* • *"and his/her heirs"*	No limitation: **Absolute** ————————	NONE ————————		
Fee Tail • *passes to issue until line runs out* • *"and the heirs of his/her body"*	*Next estate in grantor:* *Will end naturally:* **xxxx** *May end early by its own terms:* **Determinable**			
Life Estate • *ends when holder dies* • *"for life"* **Term of Years** • *lease* • *"for 10 years"*	*May be interrupted by next estate:* **Subject to a condition subsequent**			

Notice that we've connected the "NONE" entry in column 3 to the "Absolute" entry in column 2 by using arrows. You can simply follow the arrow from column 2 to the appropriate entry in column 3. (Recall that there is no such matching relationship between the entries in column 1 and those in column 2.) In other words, wherever you see an arrow in this chart, you can follow it to the appropriate entry in the next column. Where you do not see an arrow, do *not* try to connect entries across the lines.

▶ **Sample Conveyance.**

O to A and her heirs.

Columns 1 & 2:   We know that A has a *possessory estate in fee simple* (column 1) *absolute* (column 2).

Column 3:   Follow the arrow and note that O has no future interest because O conveyed everything to A.

The state of the title is this: *A has a possessory estate in fee simple absolute.*

▶ The Grantor's Future Interest Following an Estate That Ends Naturally (A Reversion)

Next we consider the grantor's future interest *following an estate that ends naturally* (a fee tail, life estate, or term of years). Recall that in Chapter 3 we used "xxxx" to designate these estates in column 2 of the chart. The name for the future interest that follows an estate that ends naturally is a **reversion**. You can remember this name because it indicates that the possessory interest in the land, which formerly was in the grantor, will revert *back* to the grantor again when A's estate naturally ends.

We say that O's reversion will "wait patiently" until A's possessory estate "ends naturally." O's reversion *will not interrupt* A's possessory estate, causing it to end earlier than it otherwise would. It waits patiently until the natural time span of the possessory estate expires. The grantor has chosen to wait patiently until the possessory estate reaches its natural end. We'll place the reversion in column 3, indicating that it "waits patiently" and using arrows to show the connection to the "xxxx" entry, like this:

Possessory Estate		First Future Interest		
❶ Nature	❷ Added Limitation	❸ Kind of Future Interest		
Fee Simple • *no inherent end* • *"and his/her heirs"*	No limitation: **Absolute** ➡	NONE		
Fee Tail • *passes to issue until line runs out* • *"and the heirs of his/her body"*	*Next estate in grantor:* *Will end naturally:* **xxxx** ➡	*In grantor:* *Waits patiently:* **Reversion**		
Life Estate • *ends when holder dies* • *"for life"*	*May end early by its own terms:* **Determinable**			
Term of Years • *lease* • *"for 10 years"*	*May be interrupted by next estate:* **Subject to a condition subsequent**			

▶ **Sample Conveyance.**

O to A for life.

Column 1:   We see that A has a *possessory estate in life estate.*

Column 2:   We know that there is no added limitation (the grantor didn't say something like "to A for life or until B marries"). So the "xxxx" entry tells us not to include a term for an added limitation.

Column 3:   We know that O has a future interest because O did not convey everything to A (A has only a life estate). Following the arrow to column 3, we see that O has the future interest that "waits patiently" until the life estate "ends naturally" (a *reversion*).

Therefore, the state of the title is this:

A has a posssessory estate in life estate;

O has a reversion.

▶ The Grantor's Future Interest Following a Determinable Estate (A Possibility of Reverter)

Remember that a determinable estate has an added limitation that might cause it to end early (e.g., ". . . until Doug graduates from college"). Recall also that in a determinable estate this limitation is placed within the language describing that estate. Look at the chart again to locate the determinable estate, with the words "May end early by its own terms" reminding you of its meaning.

The grantor's future interest following a determinable estate is called a ***possibility of reverter***.[14] Since A's estate will end automatically if the triggering event occurs, we say that O's possibility of reverter "waits patiently" to see if the event will occur. Like a reversion, O's possibility of reverter does not interrupt A's determinable estate. A's determinable estate ends upon the occurrence of the event set forth in the description of A's estate. O need do nothing but sit and "wait patiently."

---

[14] In theory, a grantor can have both a reversion (because she had a fee simple but conveyed only a smaller estate like a life estate) *and* a possibility of reverter (because she placed an added limitation on the life estate that might cause it to end early). In such a case, we call the grantor's future interest simply a reversion. The same is true if the grantor has both a reversion and a right of entry, described in the next section.

Don't confuse the possibility of reverter with a reversion (the grantor's future interest following a fee tail, life estate, or term of years).[15] A reversion is not speculative. Since it follows a fee tail, life estate, or term of years, we know that the prior estate *will* end and that the reversion *will* become possessory at some point. However, a grantor's future interest following a determinable estate often *is* speculative. The event that forms the added limitation *may or may not* occur. Therefore, we say that O has only a *possibility* of reverter.[16]

We'll add the possibility of reverter to column 3, indicating that it "waits patiently." Again, we'll use arrows to connect it to the estate it follows (the determinable estate).

Possessory Estate		First Future Interest		
❶ Nature	❷ Added Limitation	❸ Kind of Future Interest		
Fee Simple • *no inherent end* • *"and his/her heirs"*	No limitation: **Absolute** ➡	NONE		
Fee Tail • *passes to issue until line runs out* • *"and the heirs of his/her body"*	*Next estate in grantor:* *Will end naturally:* **xxxx** ➡	*In grantor:* *Waits patiently:* **Reversion**		
	May end early by its own terms: **Determinable** ➡	*Waits patiently:* **Possibility of reverter**		
Life Estate • *ends when holder dies* • *"for life"* **Term of Years** • *lease* • *"for 10 years"*	*May be interrupted by next estate:* **Subject to a condition subsequent**			

▶ **Sample Conveyance.**

O to A and her heirs so long as
the land is used for a library.

---

[15] You will sometimes see reversions, possibilities of reverter, and rights of entry referred to by the umbrella term "reversionary interests," the larger category of interests that covers all three.

[16] Take care not to confuse the two terms, even though they are so similar. In particular, don't say "possibility of reversion."

Column 1:   A has a *possessory estate in fee simple.*

Column 2:   We see that O has added a limitation requiring the land to be used for a library. The limitation uses "so long as" language and is placed in front of the punctuation marking the end of the description of A's estate. Therefore, we see that A's fee simple estate is *determinable.*

Column 3:   Since O did not convey away the future interest following A's estate, O has retained the future interest. Follow the arrow. O's interest following a determinable estate is a *possibility of reverter.* It waits patiently to see if and when the prior estate will end, that is, to see if and when the land will cease to be used for a library.

Therefore the state of the title is this:

A has a possessory estate in fee simple determinable;

O has a possibility of reverter.

▶ The Grantor's Future Interest Following an Estate Subject to a Condition Subsequent (A Right of Entry)

Recall that an estate subject to a condition subsequent might end early, but the words creating the limitation are placed in the description of the next estate. The next estate can interrupt A's estate if the described event occurs. Look at the chart again to locate the "Subject to condition subsequent" entry (column 2), with the words "May be interrupted by next estate" reminding you of its meaning.

The name for the future interest that follows an estate subject to condition subsequent is a **right of entry**. Unlike the possibility of reverter, O's right of entry would *interrupt* the prior estate if the described event occurs. The limitation is placed in the description of O's reversion. Therefore, the reversion could cause the possessory estate to end earlier than the possessory estate naturally would have ended.

It may help you to remember the name "right of entry" if you remember that when the possessory interest is subject to condition subsequent, the land does not automatically "revert" to the grantor, as it does for a determinable estate. Rather, the grantor must take some action to enforce the right to enter into possession. Therefore, we call this future interest a "right of entry." If the grantor exercises the right, the grantor can retake the land. If the grantor does nothing, possession remains in A.

We'll add the right of entry to column 3, indicating that it "interrupts the prior estate." Arrows indicate the connection to the estate it follows, the estate subject to a condition subsequent.

Possessory Estate		First Future Interest		
❶ Nature	❷ Added Limitation	❸ Kind of Future Interest		
Fee Simple • no inherent end • "and his/her heirs"	No limitation: **Absolute** ➡	NONE		
Fee Tail • passes to issue until line runs out • "and the heirs of his/her body"	*Next estate in grantor:* *Will end naturally:* **xxxx** ➡	*In grantor:* *Waits patiently:* **Reversion**		
	May end early by its own terms: **Determinable** ➡	*Waits patiently:* **Possibility of reverter**		
Life Estate • ends when holder dies • "for life" **Term of Years** • lease • "for 10 years"	*May be interrupted by next estate:* **Subject to a condition subsequent** ➡	*Interrupts prior estate:* **Right of entry**		

▶ **Sample Conveyance.**

> *O to A and her heirs; however,*
> *if the land is not used for a library, then to O.*

Column 1:   We know that A has a *possessory estate in fee simple*.

Column 2:   We see that O has added a limitation about use as a library. The limitation uses "however" language and is placed *behind* the semicolon separating A's estate from the next interest (O's interest). Therefore, we conclude that A's estate is *subject to a condition subsequent*.

Column 3:   Follow the arrow. If A's interest is subject to a condition subsequent, then O's interest is a *right of entry*. If the event occurs, O's interest will interrupt A's estate (if O so chooses).

Therefore, the state of the title is this:

A has a possessory estate in fee simple subject to a condition subsequent;

O has a right of entry.

Here is a quick summary of the grantor's future interests that follow the possessory estates:

Possessory Estate	Grantor's Future Interest
A fee simple absolute	None
A fee tail, life estate, or term of years *(whether or not it has an added limitation)*	Reversion
A fee simple determinable *(until, during, while, as long as)*	Possibility of reverter
A fee simple subject to a condition subsequent *(but if, provided that, on condition that, however)*	Right of entry

▶ Identifying the Durational Nature of the First Future Interest

We now know what *kind* of future interest will follow the possessory estate, but we need to know more than that. We need to know the duration of that future interest if and when it becomes possessory. We need this information for a future interest just as we needed it for the possessory estate (column 1). Therefore, the next column (column 4) will be another "Nature" column, identical to the "Nature" column for the possessory estate (column 1).

The choices in column 4 will be the very same choices as those in column 1:

Fee simple

Fee tail

Life estate

Term of years

We will fill in these choices on the chart, just as we did for the possessory estate. By now, you probably don't need the reminders of what the column 1 and 4 interests mean, so we'll delete these descriptions. The chart now looks like this:

Possessory Estate		First Future Interest	
❶ Nature	❷ Added Limitation	❸ Kind of Future Interest	❹ Nature
Fee Simple • "and his/her heirs"	No limitation: **Absolute** ➡	NONE	**Fee Simple** • *no inherent end* • *"and his/her heirs"*
Fee Tail • "and the heirs of his/her body"	*Next estate in grantor:*	*In grantor:*	**Fee Tail** • *passes to issue until line runs out*
Life Estate • "for life"	*Will end naturally:* **xxxx** ➡	*Waits patiently:* **Reversion**	• *"and the heirs of his/her body"*
Term of Years • "for 10 years"	*May end early by its own terms:* **Determinable** ➡	*Waits patiently:* **Possibility of reverter**	**Life Estate** • *ends when holder dies* • *"for life"*
	May be interrupted by next estate: **Subject to a condition subsequent** ➡	*Interrupts prior estate:* **Right of entry**	**Term of Years** • *lease* • *"for 10 years"*

Consider the following conveyance:

O to A and her heirs, but if A gets a divorce, then to O.

We will use the chart to identify the possessory estate and the future interest, like this:

Column 1:   First, we see that A's possessory estate is a *fee simple*. (We know that from the words "and her heirs.")

Column 2:   Then we ask whether O has added a limitation. Looking at the conveyance, we see that O has added the divorce limitation. O added "but if A gets a divorce, then to O." Look at the choices in column 2. We can rule out both "Absolute" and the four x's, since the grantor added a limitation.

      That leaves "Determinable" and "Subject to a condition subsequent." Which is this? Notice the language used for the limitation: "but if." And notice that the limitation is placed after the first comma, outside the language creating A's interest. That means that this is a "condition subsequent." So we know that A has a *pos-

sessory estate in fee simple subject to a condition subsequent.

Column 3:   Follow the arrow. We see that the future interest that follows an estate subject to a condition subsequent is called a *right of entry*. We know, of course, who owns the right of entry: the grantor (because the grantor still owns what the grantor didn't convey away).

Column 4:   What is the durational nature of O's right of entry ("then to O")? As we learned in Chapter 2, under modern law, an estate with no words of limitation is presumed to be the largest estate possible, a *fee simple*. And though we haven't yet filled in the "Added Limitation" subcolumn for the future interest, you probably can guess that this fee simple will be "absolute," since it has no added limitation.

Therefore, we know that the state of the title is this:

A has a possessory estate in fee simple subject to a condition subsequent;

O has a right of entry in fee simple absolute.

▶ Study Questions and Practice Exercises

Practice working with the material in this chapter, and learn it well before you go on to the next chapter. Answer the following questions, using the chart to help you. Make them into flash cards (*including the number of the exercise so you can identify the question later*), add them to your other cards, shuffle, and practice them all again.

4-1 What future interest remains after O conveys a fee simple absolute?

4-2 If the future interest following a life estate is in the grantor, what is it called?

4-3 If the future interest following a term of years is in the grantor, what is it called?

4-4 If the future interest following a fee simple determinable is in the grantor, what is it called?

4-5 If the future interest following a fee simple subject to a condition subsequent is in the grantor, what is it called?

4-6 If the future interest following a life estate determinable is in the grantor, what is it called?

4-7 If the future interest following a term of years subject to a condition subsequent is in the grantor, what is it called?

4-8 What is the name of the grantor's future interest that "waits patiently" for the prior estate to "end naturally"?

4-9 What is the name of the grantor's future interest that can interrupt the prior estate, causing it to end early?

4-10 A grantor can have three future interests: a reversion, a possibility of reverter, and a right of entry. Which two operate automatically, without any action by the grantor?

4-11 through 4-29 *Turn back to questions 3-11 through 3-29 on pages 35-36. There you identified the name for A's estate. Now, for each of those conveyances, add the complete name for the grantor's future interest.*

Estates Followed by Remainders

5

Up to now, we've been working only on conveyances in which the future interest is retained by the grantor. Now it's time to turn our attention to conveyances in which the grantor has conveyed not only the possessory estate but a future interest as well.

▶ Remainders

Recall that when we studied future interests retained by the grantor, we looked first at the grantor's future interest following an estate that will end naturally (a fee tail, life estate, or term of years). A grantor's future interest following such an inherently limited estate is called a reversion. We distinguished the reversion from the other two future interests held by the grantor by saying that the reversion "waits patiently" for the prior estate to end. We know that the prior estate will end eventually because it is an inherently limited estate (a fee tail, life estate, or term of years). The reversion simply "waits patiently" for that time to come. No added limitation might cause it to end early. In the "Added Limitation" column (column 2), we used four x's. Following the arrow into column 3, we saw that the grantor's future interest is a reversion. Review the chart on page 47 to remind yourself of this distinction.

Now that we are studying conveyances placing the future interest in a *second grantee*, we'll be working with the very same distinction. In this chapter, we will study the situation in which the grantor conveys an inherently limited estate (a fee tail, life estate, or term of years) and *also* conveys the future interest that follows it. For example, consider

O to A for life, then to B.

Here we see that O has conveyed an inherently limited estate (a life estate) to A. Rather than retaining the future interest that follows that life estate, however, O has conveyed it to B. If O had retained that future interest, we would have called it a reversion, but since O conveyed it to another grantee, we call it a **remainder**. A remainder is a *grantee's* future interest that "waits patiently" for the possessory estate to "end naturally." In the conveyance, the only difference between the reversion and the remainder is who holds it.

Distinguishing Remainders and Reversions

Remainder

O to A for life, <u>then to B</u>.

Reversion

O to A for life, <u>then to O</u>.

To be considered a remainder, the future interest must be conveyed to a second grantee in the same conveyance that created the possessory estate it follows. A grantor can convey a possessory estate in one conveyance, retaining a future interest (a reversion), and subsequently, in a second conveyance, transfer the reversion to a second grantee. However, the reversion doesn't change its name when it is later conveyed to a grantee. It was created as a reversion, and it remains a reversion, even though it is now held by a grantee.

We'll have to find a place on the chart for these conveyances. To do that, we'll draw a horizontal line to mark the distinction between future interests in the grantor and those in the grantee. We'll draw the line across both column 2 (the "Added Limitation" column) and column 3 (the "Kind of Future Interest" column) because, as we shall see, most of the names in both columns will be different if the future interest is conveyed to a second grantee instead of retained by the grantor.

From here on, we'll refer to column 2 limitations preceding a *grantor's* future interest as those "above the line." We'll refer to column 2 limitations preceding a *second grantee's* future interest as those "below the line." Similarly, in column 3, we'll refer to a *grantor's* future interests as those "above the line." We'll refer to a *second grantee's* future interests as those "below the line."

Notice that above the line we had already added the words "Next estate in grantor" in column 2 and "In grantor" in column 3. Now we'll add the counterparts to the columns below the line. We'll add the words

"Next estate in a grantee" below the line in column 2. Similarly, we'll add the words "In grantee" below the line in column 3. Look at the chart below and locate these horizontal lines and written reminders.

Now, we'll supplement the chart to account for these conveyances that place the future interest in a second grantee. We'll first look at column 2, the "Added Limitation" column. Above the line, recall that we indicated the lack of an added limitation by four x's, and we connected the x's with an arrow to the future interest that follows that possessory estate. We'll do exactly the same thing below the line. We'll indicate the lack of an added limitation by four x's, and we'll connect the x's with an arrow to the grantee's future interest that follows it. Both above and below the line, there is no term to indicate the *lack* of an added limitation.

Now, we move to column 3. As we have just seen, when the future interest following an inherently limited estate is conveyed to a *second grantee*, we call the future interest a ***remainder***. We'll add "Remainder" to column 3, and we'll use an arrow to connect it to the column 2 entry it follows. Now the chart looks like this:

Possessory Estate		First Future Interest		
❶ Nature	❷ Added Limitation	❸ Kind of Future Interest	❹ Nature	
Fee Simple • *"and his/her heirs"*	No limitation: **Absolute** ➡	NONE	**Fee Simple** • *no inherent end* • *"and his/her heirs"*	
Fee Tail • *"and the heirs of his/her body"* **Life Estate** • *"for life"* **Term of Years** • *"for 10 years"*	*Next estate in grantor:* *Will end naturally:* **xxxx** ➡ *May end early by its own terms:* **Determinable** ➡ *May be interrupted by next estate:* **Subject to a condition subsequent** ➡	*In grantor:* *Waits patiently:* **Reversion** *Waits patiently:* **Possibility of reverter** *Interrupts prior estate:* **Right of entry**	**Fee Tail** • *passes to issue until line runs out* • *"and the heirs of his/her body"* **Life Estate** • *ends when holder dies* • *"for life"* **Term of Years** • *lease* • *"for 10 years"*	
	Next estate in a grantee: *Will end naturally:* **xxxx** ➡	*In a grantee:* *Waits patiently:* **Remainder**		

To see how this works, we'll analyze our sample conveyance:

O to A for life, then to B.

Column 1:   A has a *possessory estate in life estate*.

Column 2:   In our expanded version of column 2, we have a horizontal line, with entries above it and below it. *The first decision we have to make is whether we will be working above the line or below the line.*

How do we know? By looking to see whether the *next* estate (the future interest following the life estate) is retained by the grantor or conveyed to a second grantee. Here we see that the future interest is conveyed to a second grantee, so we know that we must work below the line in both column 2 and column 3. Returning our attention to the possessory estate (A's estate), we observe that the grantor has not created an additional limitation, so we don't add a term (the xxxx entry).

Column 3:   Follow the arrow into column 3. Notice that following the arrow keeps us below the line, in the part of the column describing future interests conveyed to a second grantee. Following the arrow, we see that B has a future interest that "waits patiently" until the life estate ends (a *remainder*).

Column 4:   Now decide the durational nature of B's remainder once it becomes possessory. The conveyance expresses no words of limitation to tell us the durational nature of the estate B will have, so we know that the estate is presumed to be in fee simple. And after we've filled in more columns on the chart, we'll see that this fee simple, when it becomes possessory, will be "absolute," since no limitation is placed on the conveyance to B.

Therefore:

A has a possessory estate in life estate;

B has a remainder in fee simple absolute.

As a review, here is how to use the expanded version of the chart to analyze the *reversion* in the prior box:

O to A for life, <u>then to O.</u>

Column 1:   A has a *possessory estate in life estate*.

Column 2:   In our expanded version of column 2, we have a horizontal line, with entries above it and below it. *The first deci-*

sion we have to make is whether we will be working above the line or below the line.

We decide by looking to see whether the *next* estate (the future interest following the life estate) is retained by the grantor or conveyed to a second grantee. Here we see that the future interest is retained by the grantor, so we know that we must work *above* the line in both column 2 and column 3. Returning our attention to the possessory estate (A's estate), we observe that the grantor has not created an additional limitation, so we don't add a term (the xxxx entry).

Column 3:   Follow the arrow into column 3. Notice that following the arrow keeps us above the line, in the part of the column describing future interests retained by the grantor. Following the arrow, we see that O has the future interest that "waits patiently" until the life estate ends (a *reversion*).

Therefore:

A has a possessory estate in life estate;

O has a reversion in fee simple absolute.

Remainder and Reversion

Remainder
A future interest created when a grantor conveys an inherently limited possessory estate and, in the same conveyance, conveys the future interest to a second grantee.

Reversion
A future interest created when a grantor conveys an inherently limited possessory estate and retains the future interest rather than conveying it to a second grantee.

▶ Vested and Contingent Remainders

Remainders come in two kinds: **vested** and **contingent**. We will spend the rest of this chapter studying these two kinds. Here is the difference: According to the words actually creating it, a vested remainder is certain to become possessory. A contingent remainder is not.

What do we mean by this distinction? A remainder, of course, is a future interest. While someone else is holding the possessory estate (a life estate, perhaps), the remainder-holder is waiting patiently for that possessory estate to end. The remainder is vested if, according to the words creating the remainder, it will one day ripen into a possessory estate. It's just a matter of waiting until the prior life estate ends. Here's an example of a conveyance with a vested remainder:

O to A for life, then to B.

Notice that B's remainder is certain to become possessory. It's just a matter of time until A dies. B doesn't have to do anything to ensure the future possession. B doesn't even have to survive. B's remainder will become possessory even if B has already died and only B's successors are alive to enjoy it.

For a contingent remainder, however, it's not so easy. For a contingent remainder, there is some other hurdle to surmount in addition to the termination of the prior estate. What kinds of things might we be talking about?

Well, maybe when the grantor conveyed the remainder to the grantee, the grantor created a **condition precedent**—something that has to happen *before* the remainder-holder can take possession. For example, maybe the grantor specified that the remainder-holder has to be at least 25 years old when A dies:

O to A for life, then to B if B has reached 25 years old.

Or maybe the grantor conveyed the remainder to a person not yet born. For example, the grantor may have conveyed the remainder "to my first grandchild." If at the time of the conveyance the grantor does not yet have a grandchild, a grandchild must first be born before the remainder can become possessory.

Or maybe the grantor conveyed the remainder to whoever is the neonatologist at the local hospital at the time the life estate ends. But we can't be sure that there will *be* a neonatologist at the local hospital when the life estate ends, let alone know who it will be. Before the remainder can become possessory, we have to see whether there will be a person who matches the grantor's description, and we have to know who it is. If there is no one who matches the description, the grantor will have given the remainder to someone who does not exist, and, therefore, the remainder will fail.

These examples demonstrate some of the situations that cause a remainder to be contingent rather than vested. They are expressed succinctly in the following definitions of vested and contingent remainders:

Vested and Contingent Remainders

Vested

A remainder is vested if:

1. It is given to an *ascertained* person *and*

2. It is *not subject to a condition precedent* other than the natural termination of the preceding estate.

Contingent

Conversely, a remainder is contingent if:

1. It is given to an *unascertained* person *or*

2. It is subject to a *condition precedent* other than the natural termination of the preceding estate.

Memorize the two characteristics that determine whether a remainder is vested or contingent. A remainder is contingent if it is given to an unascertained person or if it has a condition precedent. Otherwise, the remainder is vested. Now, we'll explore each of these characteristics to be sure their meaning is clear.

▶ Ascertained Person

First, what do we mean by an ***ascertained*** person? A person is ascertained if he or she *has been born* and *is identified*. If the remainder is given to a person who is alive and who can be identified *now*, that person is ascertained. Our grantor's first grandchild above is not yet born. And the neonatologist at the local hospital is not yet identified. We don't know who that person will be or even whether there will be such a person at all.

Here is a conveyance in which the remainder is given to an ascertained person:

O to A for life, <u>then to Jackie Walters.</u>

Jackie Walters has been born, and she is identified by her name rather than by a description that might match someone else or no one at all. At the moment of the conveyance, we have a living person who holds the remainder, and we can tell exactly who the person is. If we had business to discuss with the holder of the remainder, we would know whom to contact. Memorize the two conditions necessary for a person to be ascertained.

> ### Two Requirements for an Ascertained Taker
>
> - Born
> - Identified

In this text, whenever we refer to someone by a letter-name, such as O, A, B, C, etc., we'll assume that the person is alive and identified. Therefore, in this text, we will assume that the remainder-holder in the following sample conveyance is ascertained:

O to A for life, <u>then to B.</u>

▶ Class Gifts

Sometimes a grantor will convey a remainder to a class of persons. For instance, O might convey "to my grandchildren." Assume that O has three grandchildren at the time of the conveyance. But if O is still alive, and especially if any of O's children are alive, O might have more grand-children after the conveyance is made. Does this mean that the remainder is contingent because there is the possibility that not all of the remainder-holders are ascertained? Or does it mean that the remainder is somehow partly vested and partly contingent?

The answer is much simpler than that. A remainder conveyed to a class is considered vested if *one* of the remainder-holders is ascertained. We'll learn more about class gifts in Chapters 7 and 14. However, for now, just remember that, in our example above, if O has even one grandchild at the time of the conveyance, the class gift is vested.

▶ Review of the Requirement That the Holder Be Ascertained

A remainder is contingent if the holder is not ascertained. Here are some conveyances in which the remainder-holder *is* ascertained:

O to A for life, <u>then to B</u>.

O to A for life, <u>then to A's first child</u>. (A has one child, B.)

O to A for life, <u>then to A's children</u>. (A has one child, B.)

O to A for life, <u>then to A's present Property teacher</u>. (A is taking Property right now from Professor X.)

Here are examples of conveyances in which the remainder-holder is *not* ascertained:

O to A for life, <u>then to A's first child</u>. (A has no children.)

O to A for life, <u>then to whoever is then teaching Property at A's alma mater</u>. (We cannot *now* know the identity of the holder.)

O to A for life, <u>then to A's widow</u>. (We cannot *now* know who will be A's widow. Even if A is presently married, A may divorce or A's spouse may die, and, therefore, A may not have a widow at all. Or A may remarry, in which case A's widow may be someone else entirely, someone unknown at the time of the conveyance.)

O to A for life, <u>then to B's heirs</u>. (We cannot *now* know who will be B's heirs. Various members of B's family may die first. B may marry or divorce or be widowed. This is why we say that a living person has no heirs. See page 4.)

▶ Condition Precedent

The other characteristic of a vested remainder is that it has no ***condition precedent***. What do we mean by a condition precedent? We saw in Chapter 3 that a condition *subsequent* is an event that might divest an interest *after* it becomes possessory. A condition *precedent* is a condition other than the ending of the prior estate that must be met *before* the remainder is ready to *become* possessory. Consider, for example, the following conveyance:

O to A for life, then to B <u>if B has reached 21</u>.

For B's remainder to become possessory, B must have reached 21 by the time A dies. If B hasn't reached 21 by the time A dies, his remainder fails before it has never become possessory. B's remainder is subject to a condition precedent. Therefore, B's remainder is not vested; it is contingent.

Remember that to make a remainder contingent, the condition must be something *other than merely the ending of the prior estate*. For instance, a remainder that follows a life estate is not contingent merely because the person who serves as the measuring life for the life estate must first die. If the need for the end of the prior estate were enough to make a remainder contingent, there would be no such thing as a vested remainder, for all remainders must "wait patiently" for the prior estate to end.

One more thing about conditions precedent: They are found within the language that creates the remainder itself.[17] They are *not* found in the description of a subsequent estate. In other words, they are found within the commas (or other punctuation marks) setting off the description of the interest they limit. For example, consider this conveyance:

O to A for life, <u>then to B if B survives A.</u>

The language describing the limiting condition ("if B survives A") is found within the punctuation marking the description of B's interest. Therefore, B's interest is subject to a condition precedent. Now, consider this conveyance:

O to A for life, <u>then to B,</u>
but if B does not survive A, then to C.

If B does not survive A, the result will be the same as the result in the prior conveyance: B's estate will never become possessory. The grantor's intent probably is identical to the intent of our first example. However, in the second example, the limiting language ("but if B does not survive A") is not found within the description of B's interest, that is, between the commas marking B's estate ("then to B"). Instead, the limiting language is found in the description of C's estate.

A limiting condition placed in an estate after *the description of the remainder it limits is not a condition precedent. It does not render the remainder contingent.* This is true even if the limiting condition could prevent the estate from ever becoming possessory.[18] Therefore,

---

[17] Occasionally, a condition precedent can be found within the description of a *prior* estate, but, typically, they are found within the description of the remainder itself. In the examples in this book, we will deal primarily with the more typical placement of the words creating the condition precedent. The important point here is that the condition precedent never *first* appears in the words describing a *subsequent* estate.

[18] In Chapter 7, we'll see that a condition that could prevent the remainder from becoming possessory but that is placed in a *subsequent* estate makes the vested remainder "subject to divestment."

as we are first learning about contingent remainders, remember to look *only within the commas* when you are checking for conditions precedent.[19] When in doubt, remember to draw vertical lines to separate the descriptions of the various estates described in the conveyance.

Condition Precedent

A condition that

▶ Is set out within the description of a particular estate and

▶ Must be satisfied before that estate can become possessory.

▶ Remainders That Are Contingent for More Than One Reason

A remainder can be contingent both because it has a condition precedent and because the holder is unascertained. If the condition precedent is subsequently satisfied but the holder remains unascertained, the remainder is still contingent. Similarly, if the holder is ascertained but the condition precedent remains unsatisfied, the remainder is still contingent. When you are working with a conveyance and with subsequent factual developments, it can be easy to forget that the resolution of only one of these vesting requirements does not render the remainder vested. Both requirements must be met before the remainder becomes vested.

▶ Adding "Vested" and "Contingent" to the Chart

We'll add "vested" and "contingent" to the chart as options under "Remainder." Also, by now, you are familiar enough with the basic possessory estates that we can delete the remaining explanations for fee simple, fee tail, life estate, and term of years. Here is our current version of the chart:

---

[19] In Chapter 13, we'll see why this distinction is important.

Possessory Estate		First Future Interest	
❶ Nature	❷ Added Limitation	❸ Kind of Future Interest	❹ Nature
Fee Simple	No limitation: **Absolute** ➡	NONE	Fee Simple
Fee Tail			Fee Tail
Life Estate			Life Estate
Term of Years	*Next estate in grantor:*	*In grantor:*	Term of Years
	Will end naturally: **xxxx** ➡	*Waits patiently:* **Reversion**	
	May end early by its own terms: **Determinable** ➡	*Waits patiently:* **Possibility of reverter**	
	May be interrupted by next estate: **Subject to a condition subsequent** ➡	*Interrupts prior estate:* **Right of entry**	
	Next estate in a grantee:	*In a grantee:*	
	Will end naturally: **xxxx** ➡	*Waits patiently:* **Remainder** • vested • contingent	

▶ Reversions Following Contingent Remainders

Notice that if O conveys a contingent remainder, an interest is left unaccounted for. Since the remainder is contingent, *someone* has the right to take possession if the contingency is not satisfied. If O has not conveyed away this unaccounted-for interest, then O has retained it, and we call it a ***reversion***.

We treat all reversions as vested because they are a retained part of O's original (vested) estate. Since all reversions are treated as vested, you do not have to say "vested" when you identify the state of the title. Just remember that all reversions are considered vested.

Here is an example of a conveyance that articulates the reversion:

O to A for life, then to B if B has graduated from college, <u>otherwise to O</u>.

Here is an example of a conveyance that does not articulate the reversion:

O to A for life, then to B if B has graduated from college.

The interests created by each of these conveyances are identical: *A has a possessory estate in life estate, B has a contingent remainder in fee simple absolute, and O has a reversion in fee simple absolute.*

Notice that at the conclusion of A's life estate the possessory estate will go *either* to B *or* to O. O's interest does not *follow* B's interest chronologically. Rather, it is an *alternative* to B's interest, like this:

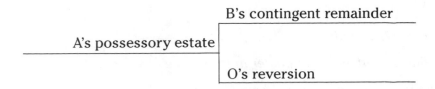

Therefore, when we use the chart to analyze this conveyance, we'll treat O's reversion in just that way: as an alternative to B's contingent remainder. Here's how:

Column 1:   A has a *life estate.*

Column 2:   (Work below the line, since the next interest is in a grantee.) The life estate has no added limitation. It will end naturally.

Column 3:   The grantee's future interest that follows an estate ending naturally is a *remainder*. This remainder is given to an ascertained taker, but it has a condition precedent (graduation from college). Therefore, the remainder is *contingent.*

Column 4:   If the contingent remainder becomes possessory, it will be a *fee simple*. And while we haven't added columns past column 4 yet, you can probably tell that if and when this fee simple becomes possessory, it will be *absolute.*

A's life estate will be followed either *by B's contingent remainder* or *by O's interest. Since O's interest (if it becomes possessory at all) will follow A's life estate rather than B's contingent remainder, we'll analyze it exactly that way. Therefore, to analyze O's interest, we'll return to columns 2 and 3, the columns that began the analysis of B's interest. In this way, we treat O's interest as an alternative to B's interest.*

Column 2:   If O's reversion does become possessory, we'll be working above the line in column 2. Since the entries in column 2 are the same for inherently limited estates (four x's), this does not change our column 2 results. It simply reminds us to follow the arrow into the correct spot in column 3.

Column 3:   Follow the arrow into column 3, where we see that O's future interest is a *reversion*. This makes sense because O's interest will become possessory, if at all, at the end of A's life estate. It is a *grantor's* future interest (above the line) following an estate ending naturally (A's life estate). Therefore, O's interest is a reversion.

Column 4:   If O's reversion becomes possessory, it will be in *fee simple absolute.*

Therefore:

A has a life estate;

B has a contingent remainder in fee simple absolute;

O has a reversion in fee simple absolute.

▶ Alternative Contingent Remainders

We'll work through the chart again, now using another conveyance. This time, instead of having O retain the future interest left over after the contingent remainder, we'll have O convey that interest to another grantee. When O conveys the future interest following a contingent remainder, that interest usually takes the form of another contingent remainder. Here is an example of a contingent remainder followed by another contingent remainder:

> **O to A for life, then to B if B has graduated from college, but if B has not graduated from college, then to C.**

Notice that at the end of A's life estate the possessory estate will go immediately either to B or to C. C's interest does not *follow* B's interest chronologically. Rather, it is an *alternative* to B's interest, like this:

```
                                          B's contingent remainder
                                        ┌──────────────────────────
              A's possessory estate     │
          _____│
                                        │
                                        └──────────────────────────
                                          C's contingent remainder
```

Notice also that the same contingency will dictate the fate of each interest. In other words, B has a remainder contingent on whether B has graduated from college. C also has a remainder contingent on whether B has graduated from college. In such a situation, we say that these are *alternative contingent remainders.*

Analyzing this conveyance using the chart, we find:

Column 1:   A has a *life estate.*

Column 2:   Since the column 3 interest is in a grantee, work below the line. A's life estate is not subject to any added limitation. It will end naturally.

Column 3:   A grantee's future interest following an estate ending naturally is a *remainder.* This remainder has a condition precedent, and, therefore, it is *contingent.*

Column 4:   If the contingent remainder becomes possessory, it will be a *fee simple absolute.*

Column 2:   Now back to column 2. If C's estate does become possessory, we'll be working below the line in column 2 (because C is a grantee, not the grantor). Therefore, we know that we will be following the arrow into column 3 below the line.

Column 3:   Following the arrow into column 3, we see that C's future interest is a *remainder,* since C's future interest will follow A's life estate (if it becomes possessory at all). A grantee's future interest following an estate ending naturally is a *remainder.* This remainder has a condition precedent (B not having graduated), and, therefore, it is *contingent.*

Column 4:   If C's contingent remainder becomes possessory, it will be a *fee simple absolute.*

Therefore:

> *A has a life estate;*
>
> *B has a contingent remainder in fee simple absolute;*
>
> *C has a contingent remainder in fee simple absolute.*

Alternative Contingent Remainders

Contingent remainders are "alternative" when they each follow the same estate and when their conditions precedent are the opposite of each other, so that the vesting of one precludes the vesting of the other.

▶ Memory Work

Memorize (1) the two characteristics that make a remainder contingent (page 57); (2) the two requirements for a vested remainder (page 57); and (3) the two requirements for a taker to be ascertained (page 58).

▶ Study Questions and Practice Exercises

Practice working with the material in this chapter, and learn it well before you go on to the next chapter. Answer the following questions, using the chart to help you. Make them into flash cards (*including the number of the exercise so you can identify the question later*), add them to your other cards, shuffle, and practice them all again.

5-1 If the future interest following a life estate is in the grantee, what is it called?

5-2 If the future interest following a term of years is in the grantee, what is it called?

5-3 If the future interest following a fee tail is in the grantee, what is it called?

5-4 What is the name of the grantee's future interest that "waits patiently" for the prior estate to "end naturally"?

5-5 How can you recognize a contingent remainder?

5-6 What two characteristics define a vested remainder?

5-7 What two characteristics define an ascertained person?

5-8 What is a condition precedent?

5-9 What are "alternative contingent remainders"?

5-10 Is a reversion deemed vested or contingent?

5-11 Is a right of entry deemed vested or contingent?

5-12 Is a possibility of reverter deemed vested or contingent?

5-13 To whom does a reversion belong?

5-14 To whom does a remainder belong?

5-15 Distinguish between a remainder and a reversion.

5-16 In column 2 on the chart, how do we decide whether to work above the line or below the line?

5-17 In column 3 on the chart, how do we decide whether to work above the line or below the line?

In the following conveyances, underline the remainder, and state whether the holder is ascertained.

5-18 O to A for life, then to B.

5-19 O to A for life, then to A's first child. (A has one child, B.)

5-20 O to A for life, then to A's heirs. (A is alive and has one child, B.)

5-21 O to A for life, then to B and her heirs. (B has no children.)

5-22 O to A for life, then to A's widow.

5-23 O to A for life, then to A's first child. (A has no children.)

5-24 O to A for life, then to this year's first-year law students at State University Law School who pass the bar.

In the following conveyances, (1) draw vertical lines marking the beginning and the end of the description of the remainder, (2) underline the remainder, and (3) state whether the remainder is subject to a condition precedent. Remember to look for the condition only within the description of the remainder itself, that is, between the two lines you have drawn.

5-25 O to A for life, then to B if B has refrained from drinking alcoholic beverages for the five years prior to A's death.

5-26 O to A for life, then to B if B has reached 21. (At the time of the conveyance, B is 22.)

5-27 O to A for life, then to B; however, if B ever drills for oil on the land, then to C.

5-28 O to A for life, then to B, on condition that B has passed the bar.

In the following conveyances, (1) draw vertical lines marking the beginning and the end of the description of the remainder, (2) underline the remainder, and (3) state whether the remainder is vested or contingent.

5-29 O to A for life, then to B, on condition that B has passed the bar. (B has been practicing law for 10 years.)

5-30 O to A for life, then to B, but if B uses the land for an insurance agency, then back to O.

5-31 O to A for life, then to B if B does not then own an insurance agency.

5-32 O to A for life, then to B if B is then married.

5-33 O to A for life, then to B; however, if B divorces after A dies, then to O.

5-34 O to A for life, then to A's surviving cousins. (A has two cousins.)

5-35 O to A for life, then to A's children. (A has one child.)

5-36 O to A for life, then to the 2001 graduates of O's law school class. (The conveyance was made in 2002.)

5-37 O to A for life, then to A's widow.

5-38 O to A for life, then to B's heirs. (B is alive.)

Do A's heirs have any property interest as a result of either of the following conveyances? If so, what is it?

5-39 O to A for life, then to A's heirs.

5-40 O to A and her heirs.

The following conveyances will help you practice the material we have studied so far. Some of these conveyances contain reversionary interests (reversions, possibilities of reverter, and rights of entry), and some contain remainders. For each conveyance, give the state of the title. Remember how to decide whether to work above the line or below the line on the chart.

5-41 O to A for life, then to B.

5-42 O to A for life, then to O.

5-43 O to A and her heirs until B reaches 25. (B is 12.)

5-44 O to A and her heirs, but if A divorces, then to O.

5-45 O to A and her heirs so long as A never uses illegal drugs.

5-46 O to A and her heirs, but if B reaches 25, then to O. (B is 15.)

5-47 O to A for life, but if an interstate highway is built within one mile of the property, then to O.

5-48 O to A for life or until A divorces, then to O.

In which of these two conveyances is B's remainder vested and in which is B's remainder contingent?

5-49 O to A for life, then to B, but if B has not graduated from college, then to C.

O to A for life, then to B if B has graduated from college, but if not, then to C.

In which of the following conveyances has O retained an interest?

5-50 O to A for life, then to B, on condition that B has passed the bar.

5-51 O to A for life, then to B.

5-52 O to A for life, then to B if B does not then own an insurance agency.

5-53 O to A for life, then to B if B has married. (B is presently married.)

5-54 O to A for life, then to B; however, if B divorces, B's estate ends.

5-55 O to A for life, then to A's surviving cousins. (A has two cousins.)

5-56 O to A for 10 years, then to B for 10 years.

5-57 O to A and the heirs of her body, then to B.

For each of the conveyances below, state whether—after the factual developments described—the remainder is vested or contingent.

5-58 "O to A for life, then to B's oldest child who survives B." Then B dies with two children living.

5-59 "O to A for life, then to A's oldest surviving child who has attained the age of 21." Then A's oldest child attains the age of 21.

5-60 "O to A for life, then to B if B marries." Then B gets married. Subsequently, B divorces.

5-61 "O to A for life, then if B has died childless, to whoever is the Dean of State University Law School at the time of A's death." Then B dies childless.

Estates Followed by Executory Interests

6

Now, it's time to finish our study of limitations followed by future interests placed in a second grantee (limitations and future interests "below the line"). In Chapter 5, we studied grantees' future interests that follow estates with *no* added limitations (remainders). Now, we'll study estates *with* added limitations and the grantees' future interests that follow them.

▶ A Determinable Estate Followed by an Executory Interest

Think back to our study of the grantor's future interests (future interests above the line). Remember that we saw that the grantor can add *to A's estate* a limitation potentially causing that estate to end early, that is, before its natural duration would otherwise cause it to end. We're talking here about limitations placed grammatically inside the description of A's estate; for example:

O to A and her heirs until B marries.

Look in columns 2 and 3, above the line, and locate the entries corresponding to this conveyance. You should be looking at the "Determinable" entry in column 2 and the "Possibility of reverter" entry in column 3.

In our example above, the grantor conveyed a determinable estate and kept the future interest for herself. But she can also convey a determinable estate and give the future interest away to someone else (a second grantee):

O to A and her heirs until B marries, then to B.

Therefore, we'll need to account for determinable estates below the line as well as above it.

The same distinguishing characteristics that applied above the line will apply below it as well. The words creating the limitation will appear *before* the comma (or other punctuation) separating the possessory estate from the next future interest. The words themselves will be words of temporal limitation, words like *until, so long as, while,* and *during.*

Above the line, we described this column 2 limitation as **determinable**. Below the line, we'll call it the same thing.[20] Therefore, an estate with an added limitation potentially causing it to end early is called a determinable estate, whether or not the next interest is in the grantor or in a second grantee.[21]

However, below the line, the *future interest* that follows a determinable estate has a different name: **executory interest**. Keep in mind that an executory interest is a future interest in a *grantee.* When the future interest following a determinable estate is in the *grantor* (O), it is called a possibility of reverter, as we saw in Chapter 4.

Except for the identity of the holder, the same characteristics describe these interests below the line as above the line. Therefore, a determinable estate ends automatically when the limiting event occurs. The second grantee (the holder of the executory interest) need not take any action to terminate the prior estate. When the limiting event occurs, that prior estate has ended, and the holder of the executory interest now automatically has the right to possession.

After adding the fee simple determinable followed by an executory interest, the chart looks like this:

---

[20] Some cases and other materials change the name of the determinable estate when the future interest is given to a second grantee rather than to the grantor. If the conveyance uses determinable language but places the next future interest in a grantee, these sources would replace the term "determinable" with the term "subject to executory limitation." For simplicity's sake, we will take the approach that does not change the name. However, if you are using other materials that do change the name or if your instructor desires, simply cross out "determinable" and write "subject to executory limitation" in this book whenever you are working below the line—that is, whenever the next future interest is in a grantee rather than the grantor.

[21] Remember that we are talking here about limitations that are placed, grammatically speaking, within the description of the estate subject to the limitation—that is, before the punctuation mark that separates the descriptions of the possessory estate and the future interest.

Possessory Estate		First Future Interest		
❶ Nature	❷ Added Limitation	❸ Kind of Future Interest	❹ Nature	
Fee Simple	No limitation: **Absolute** ➡	NONE	Fee Simple	
Fee Tail			Fee Tail	
Life Estate		*In grantor:*	Life Estate	
Term of Years	*Next estate in grantor:*		Term of Years	
	Will end naturally: **xxxx** ➡	*Waits patiently:* **Reversion**		
	May end early by its own terms: **Determinable** ➡	*Waits patiently:* **Possibility of reverter**		
	May be interrupted by next estate: **Subject to a condition subsequent** ➡	*Interrupts prior estate:* **Right of entry**		
	Next estate in a grantee:	*In a grantee:*		
	Will end naturally: **xxxx** ➡	*Waits patiently:* **Remainder** • vested • contingent		
	May end early by its own terms: **Determinable** ➡	*Waits patiently:* **Executory interest**		

▶ **Sample Conveyance.**

O to A while A serves in the United States armed forces, then to B.

Column 1:   A has a *possessory estate in fee simple.*

Column 2:   Looking ahead to the next estate, we see that the future interest is given to a second grantee (B), so we'll be choosing among the column 2 options below the line. Does this fee simple have an added limitation?

Yes. The limitation is placed in the description of A's estate rather than that of B's, and it uses words of temporal limitation ("while"). Therefore, A's fee simple is *determinable*.

Column 3:   A *grantee's* future interest following a determinable estate is an *executory interest.*

Column 4:   B's executory interest, once it becomes possessory, will be a *fee simple*. And as we'll see when we create columns beyond column 4, the fee simple is *absolute*.

Therefore:

A has a possessory estate in fee simple determinable;

B has an executory interest in fee simple absolute.

Remember that an executory interest is a future interest in a *grantee.* To clarify this distinction, let's strike out "B" in the conveyance and replace it with "O."

O to A <u>while A serves in the United States armed forces,</u> then to O.

Column 1:   A has a *possessory estate in fee simple.*

Column 2:   Looking ahead to the next estate, we see that the future interest is retained by the grantor, so we'll be choosing among the column 2 options above the line. Does this fee simple have an added limitation? Yes. The limitation is placed in the description of A's estate rather than in O's, and it uses words of temporal limitation ("while"). Therefore, A's fee simple is *determinable.*

Column 3:   A grantor's future interest following a determinable estate is a *possibility of reverter.*

Column 4:   O's possibility of reverter, once it becomes possessory, will be a *fee simple*. As we'll see when we create columns beyond column 4, the fee simple is *absolute.*

Therefore:

A has a possessory estate in fee simple determinable;

O has a possibility of reverter in fee simple absolute.

▶ Estates Subject to an Executory Limitation

Now, you know the names for an estate in which the limiting event is built into the description of the estate itself (a determinable estate) and for the grantee's future interest (an executory interest).

However, just as we saw above the line, the grantor can place the limitation in the *following future interest* instead of in the possessory estate itself. This limitation can cause the possessory estate to end early, that is, before its natural duration would otherwise cause it to end; for example:

O to A and her heirs; however if B marries, then to B.

All of the distinguishing characteristics that applied above the line, when the future interest was retained by the grantor, will apply below the line as well. The words creating the limitation will appear *after* the comma (or other punctuation) separating the possessory estate from the next future interest. The words themselves will be words of express condition—words like *but if, provided that, on condition that,* or *however.*

Above the line, when the future interest was retained by the grantor, we described this estate as "subject to a condition subsequent." Below the line, when the next interest is in a *second grantee,* we describe the estate as **subject to an executory limitation**. And the future interest that follows this estate is called an **executory interest** (the same interest that follows a fee simple determinable below the line). The "executory interest" is the limitation the possessory estate is "subject to." Therefore, for our example above, we say that *A has a fee simple subject to an executory limitation, and B has an executory interest in fee simple absolute.*

On the chart, we'll add this limitation and the future interest that follows it, like so:

Possessory Estate		First Future Interest		
❶ Nature	❷ Added Limitation	❸ Kind of Future Interest	❹ Nature	
Fee Simple	No limitation: **Absolute** ➡	NONE	Fee Simple	
Fee Tail			Fee Tail	
Life Estate			Life Estate	
Term of Years	*Next estate in grantor:*	*In grantor:*	Term of Years	
	Will end naturally: **xxxx** ➡	*Waits patiently:* **Reversion**		
	May end early by its own terms: **Determinable** ➡	*Waits patiently:* **Possibility of reverter**		
	May be interrupted by next estate: **Subject to a condition subsequent** ➡	*Interrupts prior estate:* **Right of entry**		
	Next estate in a grantee:	*In a grantee:*		
	Will end naturally: **xxxx** ➡	*Waits patiently:* **Remainder** • vested • contingent		
	May end early by its own terms: **Determinable** ➡	*Waits patiently:* **Executory interest**		
	May be interrupted by next estate: **Subject to an executory limitation** ➡	*Interrupts prior estate:* **Executory interest**		

On page 72, we saw that an executory interest that follows a determinable estate comes into possession automatically upon the occurrence of the event that forms the limitation. So does an executory interest that follows an estate subject to an executory limitation. Since the same interest (an executory interest) follows both estates, both estates end automatically upon the occurrence of the event.[22]

_____

[22] Recall that the above-the-line counterpart, the right of entry, does not automatically divest the possessory estate.

▶ **Sample Conveyance 1.**

> *O to A; <u>however, if A uses the land</u>*
> *<u>for a tavern, then to B</u>.*

Notice that the words creating the limitation ("however, if A uses the land for a tavern") appear after the punctuation ending the description of A's possessory estate. Notice also that the word "however" is one of the words of express condition in our list of examples. Use the chart to analyze this conveyance:

Column 1:   A has a *possessory estate in fee simple*.

Column 2:   Looking ahead to the next estate, we see that the future interest is given to a second grantee (B), so we'll be choosing among the column 2 options below the line. Does this fee simple have an added limitation? Yes. Is the limitation placed *outside* the description of A's estate or *inside* it? It is placed within the words that describe *B's* estate. Also it uses words of express condition ("however"). Therefore, A's fee simple is *subject to an executory limitation*.

Column 3:   Follow the arrow into column 3. Notice that we are still below the line in the area reserved for future interests conveyed to a grantee. The arrow leads directly to the grantee's future interest following an estate subject to an executory limitation: an *executory interest*.

Column 4:   B's executory interest, once it becomes possessory, will be a *fee simple*. And as we'll see when we create columns beyond column 4, B's executory interest is *absolute*.

Therefore:

    A has a possessory estate in fee simple subject to an executory limitation;

    B has an executory interest in fee simple absolute.

Remember that an executory interest is a future interest in a *grantee*. When this sort of future interest is in the grantor (O), it is called a right of entry, as we saw in Chapter 4. To clarify this distinction, let's look at two more sample conveyances.

▶ **Sample Conveyance 2.**

> *O to A; <u>however, if A uses the land for</u>*
> *<u>a tavern, then to O</u>.*

Column 1:   A has a *possessory estate in fee simple*.

Column 2:	Looking ahead to the next estate, we see that the future interest is retained by the grantor, so we'll be choosing among the column 2 options above the line. Does this fee simple have an added limitation? Yes, but the limitation is placed *outside* the description of A's estate. It is placed in the words that describe *O's* estate, and it uses words of express condition ("however"). Therefore, A's fee simple is *subject to a condition subsequent.*
Column 3:	A grantor's future interest following an estate subject to a condition subsequent is called a *right of entry.*
Column 4:	The right of entry, if and when it becomes possessory, will be in *fee simple absolute.*

Therefore:

A has a possessory estate in fee simple subject to a condition subsequent;

O has a right of entry in fee simple absolute.

▶ **Sample Conveyance 3.**

O to A and her heirs, but if A divorces, then to B.

Column 1:	We know that A's possessory estate is a *fee simple.* We can tell that from the words of limitation "and her heirs."
Column 2:	We first must decide whether we will be working above the line or below the line. We observe that the next interest is in a second grantee, so we know we'll be working below the line.
	Now we have to decide among the choices below the line. Has the grantor added a limitation to A's possessory estate? Yes. Staying below the line (because the next future interest is in a grantee), look at the choices. We can rule out the four x's, since O added an extra limitation. That leaves only two choices: "Determinable" and "Subject to an executory limitation." The limitation is placed after the comma, in the next estate, and uses the term "but if." Therefore, we know that the fee simple is *subject to an executory limitation.*
Column 3:	Following the arrow into column 3, we see that the future interest that follows a fee simple subject to an executory limitation is an *executory interest.*
Column 4:	If the executory interest becomes possessory, it will be in *fee simple absolute.*

Therefore:

A has a possessory estate in fee simple subject to an executory limitation:

B has an executory interest in fee simple absolute.

▶ Two Future Interests Held by the Second Grantee

Recall from Chapter 4 that a grantor theoretically can have two different future interests, a reversion and either a right of entry or a possibility of reverter. Consider, for example, the following conveyance:

O to A for life; but if A divorces, then to O.

O has a reversion (because A's estate is a life estate), but in theory, O also has a right of entry because A's life estate is subject to a condition subsequent. In Chapter 4, we said that we would call O's interest simply a reversion because the reversion is the larger of the two estates.[23]

The same situation can arise when both future interests are in a grantee, and we will resolve it the same way. For instance, consider

O to A for life or until A divorces, then to B.

B has a remainder (because A has only a life estate), but in theory, B also has an executory interest (because A's life estate is determinable). (Confirm this on the chart.) Because the remainder is the larger of the two future interests, we will call B's interest simply a remainder.

▶ Study Questions and Practice Exercises

Practice working with the material in this chapter, and learn it well before you go on to the next chapter. Answer the following questions, using the chart to help you. Except for 6-31 through 6-33, make the questions into flash cards (*including the number of the exercise so you can identify the question later*), add them to your other cards, shuffle, and practice them all. (If you are sure that you know the material from Chapters 1 and 2 without any hesitation, you can remove those flash cards from the stack.)

---

[23] See footnote 14 on page 42.

6-1 If the future interest following a fee simple determinable is in a second grantee, what is it called?

6-2 What do we call the future interest following a fee simple subject to an executory limitation?

6-3 What do we call a second grantee's future interest when it follows a conveyance like "to A and her heirs until B retires from the Army"?

6-4 To whom does an executory interest belong?

6-5 Distinguish between an executory interest and a right of entry or possibility of reverter.

6-6 What are the common words of temporal limitation that signal a determinable estate followed by an executory interest?

6-7 What are the common words of express condition that signal an estate subject to an executory limitation (followed by an executory interest)?

6-8 Does an executory interest take effect automatically upon the happening of the condition?

6-9 What do we call a second grantee's future interest that follows a life estate determinable?

6-10 Of the future interests following an estate with an added limitation, which is the only one that does *not* operate automatically upon the happening of the condition?

The following conveyances combine the estates and future interests we have studied so far. For each, what is the state of the title? Don't forget to draw lines to separate the descriptions of the various estates if you are unsure of your answer.

6-11 O to A and his heirs, but if A does not graduate from college, then to B.

6-12 O to A while being used as a farm.

6-13 O to A and her heirs until no longer used for a church, then to B.

6-14 O to A for life.

6-15 O to A and her heirs; however, if used for a pool hall, then to B and his heirs.

6-16 O to A and her heirs, provided that the land is always farmed.

6-17 O to A, on condition that the land is always used as a church, but if not, then to B.

6-18 O to A and the heirs of his body. (Assume the original version.)

6-19 O to A for the life of B.

6-20 O to A, but if A cuts timber on the property, then to B and her heirs.

6-21 O to A for life; however, if A rents the property, then to B and his heirs.

6-22 O to A for 25 years if A so long live.

6-23 O to A for 49 years or until the land lies fallow, whichever is first, then to B.

6-24 O to A for life, then to B.

6-25 O to A and her heirs until B reaches 25, then to B.

6-26 O to A and her heirs; however, if B reaches 25, then to B.

6-27 O to A for life or until B reaches 25, then to B.

6-28 O to A and her heirs, on condition that A does not use the property for a tavern, but if A uses the property for a tavern, then to B.

6-29 O to A, provided that the city does not change the property's zoning classification, otherwise to B.

6-30 O to A while A is attending State University, then to B.

In each of the following questions, a client has come to you for advice. Answer the client's question.

6-31 "I want to have a will that leaves all of my estate, including my house, to all of my children. However, one of my children, Timothy, is severely disabled. If my daughter Christine is willing to care for him so he doesn't have to live in an institution, I want her to be able to live with him in the house. But if the care proves to be too much for Christine and Timothy has to live in an institutional setting, then I want the house to go to all the children. They can do with it as they choose then, including selling it and dividing the proceeds or arranging for one of them to buy out the interests of the others. Is this possible?"

6-32 "My church needs to expand, and I own the property right next door. I don't need it anymore, and I'd like to donate the property to the church for as long as the church needs the space. If the church ever doesn't need the space, I'd like the property to go to the Bibb County Library. How can this be arranged?"

6-33 "My parents' wills devised their farm to my brother, Jim. The will said this: 'We give the farm to Jim for so long as Jim is farming the property. If he ever stops farming the property, we give it to our daughter, Janice.' Jim was in a car accident, and he is now permanently disabled. He can no longer farm the land. Who owns the farm now? If I (Janice) own it, what happens if I don't farm it?"

Accounting for Additional Future Interests, Class Gifts, and Subsequent Divesting

7

▶ Additional Future Interests

So far we've been working only up to the first future interest. But we are now at the point where we will need the ability to analyze more than one future interest, so it is time to venture on past column 4.

You will see that you already know what you need to know in order to navigate this new territory. As a matter of fact, all we need to do is to fill in the remaining columns just as we have filled in their counterparts for the possessory estate and for the first future interest. Columns 1, 4, and 7 are identical. Columns 2, 5, and 8 are identical. Columns 3, 6, and 9 are identical. Each interest will have a "Nature" column and an "Added Limitation" column, and each future interest will have a "Kind of Future Interest" column. Here's how the chart will look now:

Possessory Estate			First Future Interest			Second Future Interest			Third Future Interest
① Nature	**② Added Limitation**	**③ Kind of Future Interest**	**④ Nature**	**⑤ Added Limitation**	**⑥ Kind of Future Interest**	**⑦ Nature**	**⑧ Added Limitation**	**⑨ Kind of Future Interest**	
Fee Simple	No limitation: **Absolute**	➡ NONE	**Fee Simple**	No limitation: **Absolute**	➡ NONE	**Fee Simple**	No limitation: **Absolute**	➡ NONE	
Fee Tail			**Fee Tail**			**Fee Tail**			
Life Estate	_Next estate in grantor:_	➡ _In grantor:_	**Life Estate**	_Next estate in grantor:_	➡ _In grantor:_	**Life Estate**	_Next estate in grantor:_	➡ _In grantor:_	
Term of Years	_Will end naturally:_ **xxxx**	_Waits patiently:_ **Reversion**	**Term of Years**	_Will end naturally:_ **xxxx**	_Waits patiently:_ **Reversion**	**Term of Years**	_Will end naturally:_ **xxxx**	_Waits patiently:_ **Reversion**	
	May end early by its own terms: **Determinable**	_Waits patiently:_ **Possibility of reverter**		_May end early by its own terms:_ **Determinable**	_Waits patiently:_ **Possibility of reverter**		_May end early by its own terms:_ **Determinable**	_Waits patiently:_ **Possibility of reverter**	
	May be interrupted by next estate: **Subject to a condition subsequent**	_Interrupts prior estate:_ **Right of entry**		_May be interrupted by next estate:_ **Subject to a condition subsequent**	_Interrupts prior estate:_ **Right of entry**		_May be interrupted by next estate:_ **Subject to a condition subsequent**	_Interrupts prior estate:_ **Right of entry**	
	Next estate in a grantee:	➡ _In a grantee:_		_Next estate in a grantee:_	➡ _In a grantee:_		_Next estate in a grantee:_	➡ _In a grantee:_	
	Will end naturally: **xxxx**	_Waits patiently:_ **Remainder** • vested • contingent		_Will end naturally:_ **xxxx**	_Waits patiently:_ **Remainder** • vested • contingent		_Will end naturally:_ **xxxx**	_Waits patiently:_ **Remainder** • vested • contingent	
	May end early by its own terms: **Determinable**	_Waits patiently:_ **Executory interest**		_May end early by its own terms:_ **Determinable**	_Waits patiently:_ **Executory interest**		_May end early by its own terms:_ **Determinable**	_Waits patiently:_ **Executory interest**	
	May be interrupted by next estate: **Subject to an executory limitation**	_Interrupts prior estate:_ **Executory interest**		_May be interrupted by next estate:_ **Subject to an executory limitation**	_Interrupts prior estate:_ **Executory interest**		_May be interrupted by next estate:_ **Subject to an executory limitation**	_Interrupts prior estate:_ **Executory interest**	

To see how this will work, we'll revisit some prior examples, but now we'll add another future interest.

▶ **Example 1.**

> *O to A for life, then to B for life, then to C.*

As you are beginning to work with more complicated conveyances, it will help to draw vertical lines to separate the words describing each interest. Here is our example with the interests separated:

> *O to A for life, | then to B for life, | then to C.*

To identify the interests created by this conveyance, we'll simply work our way across the chart from left to right.

Column 1:	First, we see that A has a *possessory estate in life estate*.
Column 2:	We see that the next estate is in a second grantee, so we know that we will be working below the line in columns 2 and 3. In column 2, the life estate will end naturally, so we have no added limitations.
Column 3:	The estate in a second grantee that follows an estate that ends naturally is a remainder. This remainder is given to an ascertained person and has no condition precedent other than the ending of the prior estate. Therefore, B has a *vested remainder*.
Column 4:	B's remainder is in *life estate*.
Column 5:	The next future interest is in another grantee, so in columns 5 and 6 we'll be working below the line. In column 5, we see that B's remainder will end naturally (no added limitations).
Column 6:	The estate in a third grantee that follows an estate that ends naturally is a remainder. This remainder is given to an ascertained person, and it is not subject to a condition precedent. Therefore, C has a *vested remainder*.
Column 7:	C's remainder is in *fee simple*.
Column 8:	C's remainder in fee simple is *absolute*.

Therefore, the state of the title is this:

A has a possessory estate in life estate; B has a vested remainder in life estate; C has a vested remainder in fee simple absolute.

▶ **Example 2.**

> *O to A and her heirs, but if A divorces, then to B for life,*
> *then to O and his heirs.*

Here is example 2 with the estates separated:

**O to A and her heirs, | but if A divorces, then to B for life, |
then to O and his heirs.**

Column 1:   A has a *fee simple*.

Column 2:   Look to see if the next future interest will be in a grantor
or in a grantee. Here the future interest following A will
be in a grantee (B), so you know you'll be working below
the line in columns 2 and 3. For column 2, you see that
the grantor has added a limitation (no divorce) and
that the limitation uses "but if" language on the other
side of the comma. Therefore, the fee simple is *subject
to an executory limitation*.

Column 3:   The future interest that follows an estate subject to an
executory limitation is an *executory interest*.

Column 4:   If B's executory interest becomes possessory, it will be a
life estate.

Column 5:   For columns 5 and 6, check to see if the next future interest will be in the grantor or another grantee. Here it will
be in the grantor (O), so you know you'll be working
above the line in both columns. For column 5, has the
grantor added a limitation? No, so the four x's tell you
not to add a term to the name of the life estate.

Column 6:   The grantor's future interest following a life estate with
no added limitation (a life estate that will end naturally)
is a *reversion*.

Column 7:   If O's reversion becomes possessory, it will be in *fee
simple*.

Column 8:   O's fee simple will be *absolute*.

Therefore, the state of the title is this:

A has a possessory estate in fee simple subject to an executory limitation;

B has an executory interest in life estate;

O has a reversion in fee simple absolute.

▶ **Example 3.**

**O to A and his heirs until B reaches 30, then to B; however,
if B ceases to use the land for church purposes, then to C.**

Here is example 3 with the estates separated:

**O to A and his heirs until B reaches 30,
| then to B; | however, if B ceases to use the
land for church purposes, then to C.**

Column 1:   A has a *possessory estate in fee simple.*
Column 2:   The next interest will be in a grantee, so in columns 2 and 3 you'll be working below the line. In column 2, decide whether the grantor has added a limitation to the life estate. Yes, the fee simple will end if and when B reaches 30. The limitation uses the term "until," and it is placed in front of the comma, in the words describing A's interest. Therefore, the fee simple is *determinable.*
Column 3:   The grantee's (B's) future interest that follows a determinable estate is an *executory interest.*
Column 4:   B's executory interest, if and when it becomes possessory, will be a *fee simple.*
Column 5:   The next interest will be in another grantee, so in columns 5 and 6 you'll be working below the line. In column 5, ask whether the grantor added a limitation to B's fee simple. Yes, B must use the land for church purposes or lose it. The limitation is expressed with the word "however" and is placed after the semicolon. Therefore, B's fee simple is *subject to an executory limitation.*
Column 6:   C's future interest, since it follows an estate subject to an executory limitation, is an *executory interest.*
Column 7:   If and when C's future interest becomes possessory, it will be a *fee simple.*
Column 8:   C's fee simple will be *absolute.*

Therefore, the state of the title is this:

A has a possessory estate in fee simple determinable;

B has an executory interest in fee simple subject to an executory limitation;

C has an executory interest in fee simple absolute.

Now we'll add a third future interest so you can see how you can take the chart out for as many future interests as you could ever have.

▶ Example 4.

O to A for life, then to B for life, then to C, but if C sells liquor on the property, then to D.

Here is example 4 with the estates separated:

O to A for life, | then to B for life, | then to C, | but if C sells liquor on the property, then to D.

Column 1:   A has a *possessory estate in life estate.*

Column 2:   Looking ahead, we see that the next estate is in a second grantee, so we'll be working below the line. A's life estate has no added limitations ("xxxx" entry).

Column 3:   Follow the arrow into column 3 to the "Remainder" entry. Now, decide what kind of remainder this is. Is the taker ascertained? Yes. Is there a condition precedent? No. Therefore, B has a *vested remainder*.

Column 4:   B's remainder is in *life estate*.

Column 5:   Looking ahead, we see that the next estate is in a grantee, so we'll be working below the line. B's life estate has no added limitations ("xxxx" entry).

Column 6:   For C's interest, follow the arrow into column 6 to the "Remainder" entry. Now, decide what kind of remainder this is. Is the taker ascertained? Yes. Is there a condition precedent? No. Therefore, this remainder is a *vested remainder*.

Column 7:   C's remainder is in fee simple.

Column 8:   Look ahead to see who holds the next estate. Another grantee (D) does. Therefore, we know we'll be working below the line. Now, might C's estate end early? Yes. Therefore, C's vested remainder is *subject to an executory limitation*.

Column 9:   Follow the arrow into column 9, and you see that D's future interest is an *executory interest*.

Now, simply go back to an earlier future interest column that duplicates column 9 (such as column 6) and pick up from there. Use the "Second Future Interest" columns for the third future interest, imagining that they are new columns:

Column 10:   D's executory interest is *in fee simple*
Column 11:   *absolute*.

Therefore, here is the state of the title:

A has a possessory estate in life estate;

B has a vested remainder in life estate;

C has a vested remainder in fee simple subject to an executory limitation;

D has an executory interest in fee simple absolute.

You can see how you can use the chart to analyze an infinite number of future interests if you have to. Simply repeat the three columns of the "Second Future Interest" section until you finish analyzing all of the interests in the conveyance.

▶ Vested Remainders Subject to Divestment

Now that we are working with more than one future interest, we must study one more term: a vested remainder "subject to divestment."

Let's look again at example 4 above.

▶ **Example 5.**

> *O to A for life, | then to B for life, | <u>then to C</u>, | but if C sells liquor on the property, then to D.*

As we saw above, A has a life estate, B has a vested remainder in life estate, and C has a *vested remainder* (an ascertained taker and no condition precedent within the remainder's description) in fee simple *subject to an executory limitation*. D has an executory interest.

Now, we'll change our example a little bit. Rather than encouraging C not to sell liquor on the property, we'll encourage *B* not to do so.

▶ **Example 6.**

> *O to A for life, | then to B for life, | <u>then to C</u>, | but if B ever sells liquor on the property, then to D. |*

Notice that C's remainder is still vested. The limitation that B must not sell liquor on the property is not placed within the description of C's interest. Rather, it is placed within the description of the subsequent interest (D's). True, C's remainder cannot become possessory if B has sold liquor on the land, but the limitation is not placed within the words describing C's remainder. Thus, as we learned in Chapter 5, C's remainder is vested.

Despite the fact that C's remainder qualifies as vested, however, the limitation discouraging liquor sales could divest C's estate *before it ever becomes possessory*. As a matter of fact, if the limitation ever operates at all, it will prevent C's estate from becoming possessory in the first place because the limitation relates to *B's* use of the land.

When a vested remainder is burdened by an executory interest that could prevent the vested remainder from becoming possessory, we can describe that vested remainder as **subject to divestment**. It may help to think of the term "subject to divestment" as a shortened version of the longer phrase "subject to divestment *before becoming possessory*." You will be able to tell from the terms of the conveyance whether the executory interest might operate to divest the remainder before it becomes possessory.

▶ **Example 7.**

> *O to A for life, | then to B for life, | <u>then to C</u>, | but if A, B, or C ever sells liquor on the property, then to D. |*

C still has a vested remainder. Now, however, the limitation could happen *before* C's remainder becomes possessory (if either A or B sells liquor on the land during his or her life estate) or *after* it becomes possessory (if C sells liquor on the land). When a vested remainder is burdened by an executory interest that *could* prevent the vested remainder from ever becoming possessory, we still describe that vested remainder as subject to divestment.

▶ **Example 8.**

O to A for life,* | *then to B,* | *but if B divorces, then to C.

B has a vested remainder (column 3) in fee simple (column 4), but it is subject to an executory limitation in column 5. C's executory interest could divest it. Now ask yourself whether the divesting condition could happen before B's vested remainder becomes possessory. In other words, could B divorce before A dies? Yes. Even if B is not now married, he could marry and then divorce before A dies. Therefore, we can describe B's vested remainder as "subject to divestment" because it is subject to a limitation that could occur before A dies and therefore before B's estate ever has a chance to become possessory.

▶ **Example 9.**

O to A for life,* | *then to B,* | *but if B fails to give A a proper funeral within two months of A's death, then to C.

Check to see whether B's remainder is vested. Is it given to an ascertained person? Yes. Does it have a condition precedent? Look only at the underlined words—the words describing B's remainder. No condition precedent there. Therefore, B's remainder is vested.

Now, is it subject to possible divestment *before it becomes possessory*? Notice that the limitation affecting B (not giving A a proper funeral within two months of A's death) could *only* happen two months after A dies and therefore after B has taken possession. B has two months after A's death to give a proper funeral. Since this limitation could *not* end B's estate before it becomes possessory, B's vested remainder is *not* "subject to divestment." Remember, the key question is whether the vested remainder could be divested before it ever becomes possessory. If so, the remainder is subject to divestment. If not, it is *not* subject to divestment.

▶ Describing a Vested Remainder Subject to Divestment

As we have seen, a vested remainder subject to divestment is one that might be divested before it ever becomes possessory. The divesting condition can be in the form of an executory interest or even a right of entry held by the grantor. To demonstrate how to describe a vested remainder subject to divestment, we'll consider once again example 8:

> *O to A for life,* | *then to B,* | *but if B divorces, then to C.*

Use the chart to analyze this conveyance. In columns 1 and two, we see that A has a possessory estate in life estate. In columns 3, 4, and 5, we see that B has a vested remainder in fee simple subject to an executory limitation. In columns 6, 7, and 8, we see that C has an executory interest in fee simple absolute.

Now, might C's executory interest divest B's estate before it becomes possessory? Yes, B might divorce during A's life estate. Therefore, *for the column 3 entry,* add "subject to divestment" to the term "vested remainder." The complete description of B's interest is this: *B has a vested remainder (subject to divestment) in fee simple subject to an executory limitation.* This description articulates that the remainder is subject to divestment, and it identifies the kind of limitation that might cause this divestment.[24]

Now, we'll examine a remainder that might be divested by a right of entry in the grantor:

> *O to A for life,* | *then to B,* | *but if B divorces, then to O.*

Use the chart to analyze this conveyance. In columns 1 and 2, we see that A has a possessory estate in life estate. In columns 3, 4, and 5, we see that B has a vested remainder in fee simple subject to a condition subsequent. In columns 6, 7, and 8, we see that O has a right of entry in fee simple absolute.

Now, might O's right of entry divest B's estate before it becomes possessory? Yes, B might divorce during A's life estate. Therefore, *for the column 3 entry,* add "subject to divestment" to the term "vested remainder." The complete description of B's interest is this: *B has a vested remainder (subject to divestment) in fee simple subject to a condition sub-*

---

[24] You will find some disagreement among the cases and other sources about how to describe a vested remainder subject to divestment. In this, as in all other matters, follow your professor's instructions.

sequent. This description articulates that the remainder is subject to divestment, and it identifies the kind of limitation that might cause this divestment.

To avoid making the chart any more complex than it necessarily must be, this book will not add "subject to divestment" to columns 3, 6, and 9. However, if your professor wants you to include "subject to divestment" in your statement of the title, simply pencil in "subject to divestment" in these columns, as an alternative to "vested" or "contingent."

Be sure you understand the differences among a vested remainder subject to divestment before it becomes possessory, a vested remainder not subject to divestment before it becomes possessory, and a contingent remainder. These differences will become important in the chapters ahead. Just remember to take the simple steps we used in the examples above.

Identifying Contingent Remainders, Vested Remainders, and Vested Remainders Subject to Divestment

1. Draw lines separating the descriptions of the various estates.

2. Underline the remainder you're interested in.

3. Look in the underlined words for a condition precedent. If there is a condition precedent in the underlined words, the remainder is contingent. If there is no condition precedent there, the remainder is vested.[25]

4. If the remainder is vested, you have one more step to take. Look at the *next* estate. If you find a limitation that *could* divest the remainder *before it becomes possessory,* then add the term "subject to divestment" to the term "vested remainder."

▶ Vested Remainders Subject to Open

Recall from Chapter 5 that a remainder can be given to a class of persons, such as "A's children." If A has no children at the time of the conveyance, the remainder is contingent (because we have no identified takers and therefore the remainder-holders are not ascertained). However, if A has at least one child (B), the remainder is vested.[26] The remainder is vested because we have at least one identified person (B) who holds the remainder.

---

[25] Assuming it is given to an ascertained taker.
[26] Assuming no condition precedent.

The class of "A's children" could expand, though. Since A is alive, A could have more children. We describe a vested remainder that is given to a class that could expand as **subject to open**. The class is "open" for the admission of additional class members. Therefore, we can say that B has a vested remainder subject to open.[27]

If A is dead, however, A cannot have more children. In that case, the class is **closed**. You do not have to include the term "subject to open" or "closed" when you identify the state of the title unless your professor instructs you otherwise, but you should understand the terms and what they mean. We'll be working with this distinction again in Chapters 13-15.

▶ Study Questions and Practice Exercises

Practice working with the material in this chapter, and learn it well before you go on to the next chapter. Answer the following questions, using the chart to help you. Make them into flash cards (*including the number of the exercise so you can identify the question later*), add them to your other cards, shuffle, and practice them all.

7-1 What does it mean to say that a vested remainder is subject to divestment?

7-2 What does it mean to say that a remainder is "subject to open"?

7-3 What does it mean to say that a remainder given to a class is "closed"?

For each of the following conveyances, state whether B's remainder is (1) contingent, (2) vested subject to divestment before becoming possessory, or (3) vested and not subject to divestment before becoming possessory.

7-4 O to A for life, then to B, but if B ever owns an insurance agency, then to O.

7-5 O to A for 10 years, then to B for life if B has never owned a tavern, then to C.

7-6 O to A for two years, then to B, but if B ever uses the land for an insurance agency, then to C.

---

[27] A synonym for "subject to open" is "**subject to partial divestment**." The term refers to the fact that B presently has the total remainder interest. But if the class expands, B will no longer have the total interest. B's interest will have to be shared with new class members and thus will be reduced in direct proportion to the number of class members added. B's interest, however, can never be reduced to zero, no matter how many new class members are added. Therefore, we can say that B's remainder is "subject to *partial* divestment."

7-7 O to A for life, then to B, but if the city ever annexes the land, then to C.

For each of the following conveyances, state whether the underlined remainder given to a class is subject to open or closed.

7-8 O to A for life, *then to A's children.* (A has one child, B.)

7-9 Conveyance in a testator's will: T (Testator) to A for life, *then to T's children.* (T has one child, B.)

7-10 O to A for 10 years, *then to the 2001 graduates of State University Law School.* (The conveyance was made in 2002.)

7-11 O to A for life, *then to B's children.* (B presently has 3 children.)

The following conveyances will give you practice with complex conveyances. These are about as complicated as you are ever likely to see. For each, what is the state of the title? Use the chart, and do these just for fun.

7-12 O to A for life, then to B for life, then to C and her heirs; however, if C ever uses the land for a rental, then to O.

7-13 O to A for 10 years, then to B and her heirs, but if B divorces, then to C after A's estate has ended and until C ceases to live on the property, then to D.

7-14 O to A for life, then to B and his heirs while B is using the property for a law office, then to C; however, if C does not marry by age 35, then C's estate ends.

7-15 O to A for life, then to B if B survives A, but if B does not survive A, then to C if C has survived A, but if neither B nor C has survived A, then to D.

7-16 O to A for life, then to B for life as long as B does not divorce, but if B divorces, then on or after the ending of A's estate, to C for the life of B. (B has not yet divorced.)

7-17 O to A for life, then to B for 10 years, then to C's children, but if none of C's children are then living, to D. (C is alive and has one child, X, at the time of the conveyance.)

7-18 O to A for life, then to B if B has married, but if B has never married, then to C for two years, then to D and her heirs. (At the time of the conveyance, B is married.)

Shifting and Springing Executory Interests

8

Now that we can use the chart to analyze more than one future interest, we are ready to finish studying executory interests. We will study the two kinds of executory interests: **shifting** and **springing**. The difference is this:

> A **shifting** executory interest *follows* an estate in a *grantee*.

> A **springing** executory interest *divests* an estate in the *grantor*.

All of the executory interests we have seen so far have been *shifting* executory interests. Recall that all of them have *followed* an estate in a *grantee*. For instance:

**O to A, <u>but if A ceases using the land
for a church, then to B</u>.**

Notice that B's executory interest follows an interest in A (a grantee). Look back through Chapter 6, and examine each of the examples of executory interests there. In each of them, the executory interest follows an estate in a grantee. Therefore, the only new kind of future interest we will study in this chapter is the *springing* executory interest. We have already studied the *shifting* executory interest without learning its name.

Before we study the springing executory interest, we'll add both terms to the "Kind of Future Interest" columns so we can work with them there. Locate them on our final version of the chart:

	Possessory Estate			First Future Interest			Second Future Interest			Third Future Interest
	① Nature	**② Added Limitation**	**③ Kind of Future Interest**	**④ Nature**	**⑤ Added Limitation**	**⑥ Kind of Future Interest**	**⑦ Nature**	**⑧ Added Limitation**	**⑨ Kind of Future Interest**		
	Fee Simple	No limitation: **Absolute**	NONE →	**Fee Simple**	No limitation: **Absolute**	NONE →	**Fee Simple**	No limitation: **Absolute**	NONE →		
	Fee Tail	*Next estate in grantor:*	*In grantor:*	**Fee Tail**	*Next estate in grantor:*	*In grantor:*	**Fee Tail**	*Next estate in grantor:*	*In grantor:*		
	Life Estate	*Will end naturally:* xxxx	*Waits patiently:* Reversion →	**Life Estate**	*Will end naturally:* xxxx	*Waits patiently:* Reversion →	**Life Estate**	*Will end naturally:* xxxx	*Waits patiently:* Reversion →		
	Term of Years	*May end early by its own terms:* **Determinable**	*Waits patiently:* **Possibility of reverter** →	**Term of Years**	*May end early by its own terms:* **Determinable**	*Waits patiently:* **Possibility of reverter** →	**Term of Years**	*May end early by its own terms:* **Determinable**	*Waits patiently:* **Possibility of reverter** →		
		May be interrupted by next estate: **Subject to a condition subsequent**	*Interrupts prior estate:* **Right of entry** →		*May be interrupted by next estate:* **Subject to a condition subsequent**	*Interrupts prior estate:* **Right of entry** →		*May be interrupted by next estate:* **Subject to a condition subsequent**	*Interrupts prior estate:* **Right of entry** →		
		Next estate in a grantee:	*In a grantee:*		*Next estate in a grantee:*	*In a grantee:*		*Next estate in a grantee:*	*In a grantee:*		
		Will end naturally: xxxx	*Waits patiently:* **Remainder** • vested • contingent →		*Will end naturally:* xxxx	*Waits patiently:* **Remainder** • vested • contingent →		*Will end naturally:* xxxx	*Waits patiently:* **Remainder** • vested • contingent →		
		May end early by its own terms: **Determinable**	*Waits patiently:* **Executory interest** →		*May end early by its own terms:* **Determinable**	*Waits patiently:* **Executory interest** →		*May end early by its own terms:* **Determinable**	*Waits patiently:* **Executory interest** →		
		May be interrupted by next estate: **Subject to an executory limitation**	*Interrupts prior estate:* **Executory interest** • shifting • springing →		*May be interrupted by next estate:* **Subject to an executory limitation**	*Interrupts prior estate:* **Executory interest** • shifting • springing →		*May be interrupted by next estate:* **Subject to an executory limitation**	*Interrupts prior estate:* **Executory interest** • shifting • springing →		

▶ Review of Shifting Executory Interests

Now that the terms are included on the chart,[28] we'll work through one more example of a *shifting* executory interest, just to be sure you're comfortable with it before we examine a springing interest.

O to A, provided that if A ever allows the timber to be cut, then to B.

Work your way across the chart:

Column 1: A's possessory estate is in *fee simple.*

Column 2: A's fee simple may end early, and the estate that will follow it is in a grantee, so we'll work below the line. Our two choices are "Determinable" and "Subject to an executory limitation." To choose, ask whether the potentially divesting limitation is placed in A's part of the conveyance (before the first comma) or in B's part (after the comma). Ask also whether the words introducing the divesting limitation are words of temporal limitation (for example, "until") or words of express condition (for example, "but if"). The answers to these questions tell us that A's fee simple is *subject to an executory limitation.*

Column 3: Since A's fee simple is subject to an executory limitation, we know that B's future interest is an executory interest. Is it shifting or springing? Whom might it divest? Since it would divest a grantee (A), it is a *shifting executory interest.*

Column 4: If B's shifting executory interest becomes possessory, it will be in *fee simple*

Column 5: *absolute.*

▶ Springing Executory Interests

Now consider a *springing* executory interest. As we saw above, a springing executory interest divests O (the grantor), not a grantee. Here is an example:

O to A when she turns 21.

Work your way across the chart, but look carefully. Who has the possessory (present) estate? Who is entitled to possession right now? A will not take possession until she turns 21. Remember that O still has anything that O hasn't conveyed to someone else. Therefore, *O* has the possessory estate.

---

[28] The classic springing executory interest *interrupts* O's estate. Therefore, we'll place the terms "shifting" and "springing" only under the entry for executory interests that interrupt the prior estate since that is where you'll need to distinguish between shifting and springing interests. For purposes of our study, you can assume that executory interests that "wait patiently" are shifting interests.

Column 1:   O's possessory estate is in *fee simple*.
Column 2:   Now, go to column 2, and ask yourself whether you will be working above the line or below the line. Remember how to decide. Is the *next* estate in the grantor or in a grantee? Here the next estate is in a grantee (A). Therefore, work below the line.

You know that the column 2 entry is not the four x's (giving A a remainder) because O's estate is a fee simple rather than an inherently limited estate like a life estate. Therefore, your only column 2 choices are "Determinable" and "Subject to an executory limitation." Is the condition that might cause O's estate to end stated in a description of O's estate? No. The conveyance doesn't even contain a description of O's estate. Rather, the condition is placed within the description of A's estate. Therefore, O's fee simple is *subject to an executory limitation.*

Column 3:   Now follow the arrow to column 3, where you see that A's interest is an executory interest. Is it shifting or springing? The key question is, Whom does A follow? If A follows a grantee, he has a *shifting* executory interest. But if A divests O, he has a *springing* executory interest. Here A divests O, so he has a *springing executory interest*

Column 4:   *in fee simple*
Column 5:   *absolute.*

Here is the state of the title:

O has a possessory estate in fee simple subject to an executory limitation;

A has a springing executory interest in fee simple absolute.

The prior example showed a situation in which O did not convey the *possessory* estate in the conveyance. Rather, O kept the possessory estate while waiting to see if A would turn 21. A grantor also can create a springing executory interest by conveying the possessory estate in such a way that there is a gap between interests. Consider this conveyance:

O to A for life, then to B 5 years after A's death.

We see that A has a *possessory estate in life estate*. Moving to column 2, we see that A's life estate will end naturally (xxxx), but we need to know whether we are working above or below the line. Is the next estate going to be in a grantee or in the grantor?

If you are tempted to say that the next estate is in a grantee (B), look again. Notice the gap between the end of A's life estate and the beginning of B's interest. Where is the possessory estate going to be for the 5 years after A's death? In O, of course, since O did not convey away the future interest for those 5 years. So when you move into column 2, you are looking ahead to O's interest, not to B's interest. Therefore, you are working *above* the line.

Now, go to column 3, working above the line. We see that O's interest is a *reversion,* since it follows an estate ending naturally. Since we have no words indicating a lesser estate, we presume that O's reversion will be in *fee simple* (column 4).

Now, move to column 5. Is O's reversion in fee simple *absolute*? No, since it will be cut short by B's interest 5 years later. Therefore, we must decide whether to work above the line or below the line. Who owns the next estate, the estate that will follow O? The answer is B. Since the next estate is in a grantee, we know that we are working below the line. O's fee simple will end early (5 years after A's death), and the limitation is placed in the description of B's estate (not O's), so O's reversion in fee simple is subject to an *executory limitation.*

In column 6, we see that the second future interest, the interest in B, is an executory interest. Is it shifting or springing? Since B's interest divests O, a grantor, B has a *springing executory interest.* When B's interest becomes possessory, it will be a *fee simple* (column 7) *absolute* (column 8).

Therefore, the state of the title is this:

A has a life estate;

O has a reversion in fee simple subject to an executory limitation;

B has a springing executory interest in fee simple absolute.

▶ Study Questions and Practice Exercises

Practice working with the material in this chapter, and learn it well before you go on to the next chapter. Answer the following questions, using the chart to help you. Make them into flash cards (*including the number of the exercise so you can find the questions later*), add them to your other cards, shuffle, and practice them all again.

8-1 Which kind of executory interest divests the grantor?

8-2 Which kind of executory interest follows a grantee?

Many of the following conveyances contain an executory interest, but some do not. For each conveyance, state the title; that is, state the complete name of every interest held by someone. Where the conveyance contains an executory interest, distinguish between shifting and springing executory interests.

8-3   O to A; however, if B obtains her Ph.D., then to B and her heirs.

8-4   O to A for life, then to A's oldest child for life, provided that if B should join a cult during either of the life estates, then to C for life. (A has no children.)

8-5   O to A when A reaches 30. (A is 16.)

8-6   O "to my brother if and when he survives his wife."

8-7   O to A for life, then to B, on condition that B never uses illegal drugs, and if B uses illegal drugs, then his interest will cease and be replaced by an estate to C and her heirs.

8-8   T devises "to A for life, then to B, but if B should ever use the property as a rental, then to C."

8-9   O to A for 2 years, then to B if B clears the property of all of the garbage A leaves behind.

8-10   O to A for life, then to B and her heirs if B probates A's estate.

8-11   O to A for life, then one day later, to C and his heirs.

8-12   O to A for life, then to A's youngest son for life or until he ceases to use the property for his primary residence. (A has two sons.)

8-13   O to A for 10 years, then to B, provided that B never allows a meeting of the Green Party to occur on the property.

8-14   O to A for life, then to B if B delivers a eulogy at A's funeral.

Review of Future Interests in a Second Grantee and the Estates They Follow

9

Future interests in a second grantee (and the limitations that precede them) can be confusing. Even if you understand them in isolation, you can easily become confused when you try to put all of the concepts together. Therefore, here is a review to help you practice identifying these interests.

▶ Remainders

1. A remainder can follow only an inherently limited estate like a life estate, fee tail, or term of years.

2. If an inherently limited estate also has an added limitation (like a life estate determinable), the following grantee's future interest is still called a remainder. We do not say that the second grantee has both a remainder and an executory interest. The remainder is the larger of these two future interests, so we think of the remainder as including the executory interest.

3. A remainder conveyed to an unascertained taker is contingent. An unascertained taker is one who is not yet born or not yet identified.

4. A remainder-holder is not yet identified if we cannot yet tell exactly which human being will be entitled to the remainder. For example, if the remainder is given to "whoever is then the executive director of the Red Cross," the remainder-holder is not identified.

5. A remainder that has a condition precedent placed in its own description (or in the description of a prior estate) is contingent. An example of a condition precedent placed inside the description of the remainder is "O to A for life, *then to B if B survives A*." An example of a condition precedent placed in the description of a prior estate is "O to A and his heirs, but if A divorces, then to B for life, then to C and his heirs." An example of a condition precedent implicit in the description of a prior estate is "O to A for life, then to B if B survives A, *then to C*."

▶ Executory Interests

1. An executory interest is held by a grantee and follows a fee simple that might end early, either by a condition added to its own description (a fee simple determinable) or by a condition placed in the description of the executory interest that follows it (a fee simple subject to an executory limitation). An example of a fee simple determinable followed by an executory interest (in italics) is "O to A for as long as A lives on the property, *then to B*." An example of a fee simple subject to an executory limitation followed by an executory interest is "O to A, *but if A ceases to live on the property, then to B*."

2. Executory interests are either shifting or springing. A shifting executory interest follows an estate in another grantee. An example of a shifting executory interest is "O to A, *but if B graduates from law school, then to B*."

3. A springing executory interest divests an estate in the grantor. Often the grantor's intervening estate is unstated in the conveyance. Two examples of springing executory interests (in italics) are "*O to A when she marries*" and "O to A for life, *then two years later, to B*." In each, notice that O has an unstated interest that precedes the springing executory interest.

▶ Vested Remainders Subject to Divestment

1. A vested remainder subject to divestment is a vested remainder that *might* be divested before it has a chance to become possessory. The condition that might divest it is stated in the description of an estate that follows the remainder. An example of a vested remainder subject to divestment is "O to A for life, *then to B*, but if B does not survive A, then to C." The divesting condition could *prevent* the remainder from becoming possessory in the first place.

2. A vested remainder that might fail *but only after it has become possessory* is a vested remainder subject only to an executory limitation.

It is not subject to divestment before it becomes possessory. An example of a vested remainder subject only to an executory limitation is "O to A for life, *then to B*, but if B uses the land for a tavern, then to C." The divesting condition could not prevent the remainder from becoming possessory. It could only cause it to end after it had become possessory.

3. A contingent remainder is not "subject to divestment" because it isn't yet vested. It makes no sense to speak about its being "divested" before it has become "vested."

▶ Examples

Consider these three conveyances:

1. *O to A for life, then to B if B has reached 30, but if B has not reached 30, then to C.*

2. *O to A for life, then to B, but if B has not reached 30, then to C.*

3. *O to A for life, then to B, but if B ceases using the land for a farm, then to C.*

▶ **Conveyance 1.**   B's interest is a *contingent remainder* (column 3) *in fee simple* (column 4) *absolute* (column 5). It is contingent because it cannot become possessory unless B has reached 30 by the time A dies *and* the language creating this condition is found within the description of the remainder itself ("then to B *if B has reached 30*").

▶ **Conveyance 2.**   B's interest is a *vested remainder* (subject to divestment) (column 3) *in fee simple* (column 4) *subject to an executory limitation* (column 5). The language creating B's remainder has no condition precedent within it. However, in the words describing the *next* interest, the conveyance gives us a condition that, if not met, will prevent B's interest from becoming possessory. Since this condition is within the words creating the *next* interest but might cause B to lose the remainder before it ever becomes possessory, B's vested remainder is *subject to divestment*. It is subject to being divested by its *executory limitation* before ever becoming possessory.

▶ **Conveyance 3.**   B's interest is a *vested remainder* (column 3) *in fee simple* (column 4) *subject to executory limitation* (column 5). Here the conveyance contains no language that could divest B's remainder *before it becomes possessory*, either within the words creating B's interest or after them. The only condition that could divest B could not happen until *after* B's interest has already become possessory. B can cease using the land as a farm only *after* B has had an opportunity to possess the land in the first place. Since B does not have to comply with any condition before his estate becomes possessory (but must comply with a post-possession condition), B's estate is a vested remainder subject to executory limitation, but it is not subject to divestment.

Review: Remainders and Executory Interests

Vested remainder:

> *O to A for life, **then to B and her heirs**.*

Vested remainder followed by another vested remainder:

> *O to A for life, **then to B for life,
> then to C and her heirs**.*

Vested remainder (subject to divestment) (column 3) in fee simple (column 4) subject to an executory limitation (column 5):

> *O to A for life, **then to B**, but if B
> is not then living, to C.*

Another vested remainder subject to divestment (column 3) in fee simple (column 4) subject to an executory limitation (column 5):

> *O to A for life, **then to B**, but if B divorces, then to C.*

Contingent remainder:

> *O to A for life, **then to B if B is then living**.*

Contingent remainder followed by an alternative contingent remainder:

> *O to A for life, **then to B if B is then living, but if B is not then
> living, then to C**.*

▶ Study Questions and Practice Exercises

Practice working with the material in this chapter, and learn it well before you go on to the next chapter. Give the state of the title for the following conveyances, using the chart to help you. Make them into flash cards (*including the number of the exercise so you can identify the question later*), add them to your other cards, shuffle, and practice them all again.

9-1 O to A for life, then to B and his heirs, then to C and his heirs.

9-2 O to A for life, then to B's heirs, then to C's heirs.

9-3 O to A and her heirs as long as the land is used for educational purposes.

9-4 O to A for 10 years, then to B, but if B has not yet graduated from law school, then to C.

9-5 O to A and her heirs as long as the land is used for educational purposes, but if the land is not used for educational purposes, then to B and his heirs.

9-6 O to A for 5 years, then to B, but if, after taking possession, B ever fails to place a red rose on A's grave on A's birthday, then to C.

9-7 O to A and her heirs, but if she stops using the land for educational purposes, then to O.

9-8 O to A if she graduates from law school. (A has not yet graduated from law school.)

9-9 O to A for life, then to B if B survives A, but if B does not survive A, to C's children. (C has no child.)

9-10 O to A for life, then to B, but if B ever allows A to be moved into a nursing home, then to C.

9-11 Same as 9-9, but assume that C has a child, X.

9-12 First conveyance: *O to A for life, then to B and her heirs.*
Second conveyance: *A to C.*
Now classify the estates and interests.

9-13 O to A for life, then to the person who is then Dean of O's law school.

9-14 O to A for life, then to B if B is then married to C. (B is married to C.)

9-15 O to A for life, then to B, but if B does not serve as the executor of A's estate, then to C.

9-16 O to A for life, then to B if B adopts A's surviving children.

9-17 O to A, but if A mines the property, then to B and her heirs.

What Is the State of the Title?

10

As you already know, this question is a common way of asking you to identify the names of the various estates and future interests that may be represented in a particular conveyance. Now that we have covered all of the necessary terms *and if you are feeling comfortable with what each term means*, you might find it helpful to begin to organize your answers to that question by using the following list of possible answers. You'll want to do this especially if your professor plans to test you using this kind of format for your answers.

NAMING AN INTEREST

Kind of Interest	Nature of Interest	Added Limitation
1. Possessory estate	1. Fee simple	1. Absolute/no limitation
2. Reversion	2. Fee tail	2. Determinable
3. Possibility of reverter	3. Life estate	3. Subject to a condition subsequent
4. Right of entry	4. Life estate pur autre vie	4. Subject to an executory limitation
5. Vested remainder	5. Term of years	5. Subject to open
6. Vested remainder subject to divestment		
7. Contingent remainder		
8. Shifting executory interest		
9. Springing executory interest		

You'll need to select an entry from each of the columns. Once you've done that, you will have accounted for all of the kinds of information necessary to identify each individual interest.

Consider, for example, the following conveyances:

O to A for life, then to B for 10 years, then to C.

For A's interest, you would select "Possessory estate" from the first list, "Life estate" from the second list, and "Absolute/no limitation" from the third list.[29] If you want a quick way to compare answers with your classmates, you can just use the numbers. You would make similar decisions for B's interest and for C's interest. B has a *vested remainder in a term of years* (5-5-1) and C has a *vested remainder in fee simple absolute* (5-1-1).

Here is an example of a class gift subject to open:

O to A for 5 years, then to A's children.

[A has 1 child.]

A's interest is a *possessory estate in a term of years*. For A's interest, you would select "Possessory estate" from the first list, "Term of years" from the second list, and "Absolute/no limitation" from the third list (1-5-1). You would make similar decisions for the interest given to A's child. You would say that A's child has a "*vested remainder in fee simple* subject to open (5-1-5)."

Here is an example of an interest subject to divestment:

O to A for life, then to B, but if B divorces, then to C at the end of A's estate.

A's interest is a *possessory interest in life estate* (1-3-1). B has a *vested remainder subject to divestment in fee simple subject to an executory limitation* (6-1-4).[30] C, of course, has a *shifting executory interest in fee simple absolute* (8-1-1).

---

[29] Your answer would be 1-3-1. Your professor might choose to design your examination in this format, for ease of grading.

[30] B could divorce before A dies, thus divesting B's interest before it ever becomes possessory.

▶ Optional Practice

For practice in using these lists to prompt you, you can use any sample conveyance in this book.

Post-Conveyance Factual Developments

11

Up to now, we have been working only with original conveyances. We have learned to classify estates and future interests at the time of the conveyance, but we have not considered the effect of factual developments subsequent to the conveyance.

But a number of post-conveyance factual developments can affect possessory estates and future interests. For instance, remember that a future interest is a *presently existing right*, not a mere expectancy. Our system of Property law treats such a presently existing right as an "item" of property unto itself. Therefore, in most cases, a future interest can be sold, given away, or devised under a will.

In this chapter, we will consider the most common post-conveyance developments: the death of a holder, the removal of a contingency, the ascertainment of a previously unascertained remainder-holder, the subsequent conveyance of an interest, the continuation of a contingency, and the vesting in possession of a future interest. Keep in mind that the concepts and doctrines described in this chapter come into play only if you are given an original conveyance *and* one or more factual developments occurring *after* that conveyance.

Some Property classes do not have time to cover merger or destruction of contingent remainders. If your course will not cover one or both of those doctrines, simply skip that section. The answers for the Study Questions and Practice Exercises in Appendix C will identify which questions to skip.

▶ Deaths

Originally, many interests in land were not inheritable or devisable. However, today nearly all interests in land are inheritable and devisable. The death of the interest-holder does not affect the interest unless the interest, by its very nature, ends upon the holder's death. A life estate is not inheritable or devisable because it ends upon the holder's death (assuming that the holder is the measuring life).[31] A fee tail is not inheritable or devisable because it automatically passes to the holder's issue. We will treat all other possessory estates and future interests as inheritable and devisable.

What does this mean for our purposes? It means that if you are working with a conveyance and subsequently the grantor or one of the grantees dies, the interest of the deceased person (if other than a life estate or fee tail) will pass by will or by intestate succession to that person's heirs or devisees. The interest does not simply end unless it was a life estate measured by the life of the deceased. Consider this example:

O to A for life, then to B for life, then to C.

First, identify the interests. You should conclude that this is the state of the title:

A has a possessory estate in life estate;

B has a vested remainder in life estate;

C has a vested remainder in fee simple absolute.

What if A dies? Since A had a life estate, the estate simply ends, and B's future interest becomes the possessory estate. This is then the state of the title:

B has a possessory estate in life estate;

C has a vested remainder in fee simple absolute.

What if B dies before A dies? B's remainder in life estate simply ends. The state of the title is this:

A has a possessory estate in life estate;

C has a vested remainder in fee simple absolute.

---

[31] A life estate pur autre vie can be devised or inherited. Of course, it will end on the death of the measuring life.

Therefore, we see that a future interest in life estate can end before it has a chance to become possessory.

What if, before either A or B dies, C dies with a will devising all her property to D? Since C's remainder was in fee simple, it does not end merely because C dies. Rather, it passes to D. D holds the vested remainder and continues waiting for A and B to die.

Now consider this conveyance:

> *O to A for life, then to B, but if B ever*
> *divorces, then to C.*

First, identify the interests. You should conclude that after the conveyance this is the state of the title:

A has a possessory estate in life estate;

B has a vested remainder (subject to divestment) in fee simple subject to an executory limitation;

C has a shifting executory interest in fee simple absolute.

What if C dies? C had a future interest that would come into possession only upon the happening of a contingency (B divorcing). As remote and intangible as this interest may seem, the interest still passes to C's heirs or devisees.

It may seem strange to think that a future interest, especially a distant and contingent future interest, can pass by will or by intestate succession. You may be thinking that only tangible property can be inherited or devised. However, in most cases, future property rights can be passed to heirs or devisees just as readily as present rights. The future interest is itself an "item of property." A common metaphor for these multiple interests in property is the bundle of sticks. Think of the possessory estate as one of the sticks in the bundle and each future interest as another stick. The holder of nearly any of those sticks can sell it, devise it, or allow it to pass by intestate succession.

▶ Removal of Contingencies

What happens to the state of the title when a designated event either happens or can no longer happen? Consider the following conveyance:

> *O to A and her heirs, but if A divorces,*
> *then to B and his heirs.*

As always, first identify the state of the title at the time of the conveyance. You should decide that the state of the title is this:

A has a possessory estate in fee simple subject to an executory limitation;

B has a shifting executory interest in fee simple absolute.

What if A divorces? A's possessory estate ends, and B has a possessory estate in fee simple absolute.

What if A dies without divorcing? After A's death, A can no longer divorce, so the executory interest can never become possessory. It is struck, and A's heirs or devisees have a possessory estate in fee simple absolute. B has nothing.

Now consider this example:

O to A, but if A ever uses the land for a tavern, then to B.

First, identify the interests. You should conclude that this is the state of the title:

A has a possessory estate in fee simple subject to an executory limitation;

B has a shifting executory interest in fee simple absolute.

What if A dies without using the land for a tavern? B's executory interest can interrupt the possessory estate only if *A* uses the land for a tavern. Since A cannot use the land for a tavern (or anything else, for that matter) after her death, the executory interest can never become possessory. It is struck, and A's heirs or devisees have a possessory estate in fee simple absolute. Can A's heirs or devisees use the land for a tavern? Yes. They have a fee simple absolute. The condition applied only to A.

A slight change in this conveyance would make a significant difference, however. Consider this conveyance:

O to A, but if the land is ever used for a tavern, then to B.

Again, this is the state of the title:

A has a possessory estate in fee simple subject to an executory limitation;

B has a shifting executory interest in fee simple absolute.

What if A dies without using the land for a tavern? B's executory interest can interrupt the possessory estate if *anyone* ever uses the land for a tavern. Since the land could still be used for a tavern after A's death, the executory interest can still become possessory. It continues to burden the possessory estate.[32] Therefore, A's death does not affect the status of B's executory interest.

▶ Subsequent Vesting of a Contingent Remainder

As you know, a remainder is contingent if its taker is unascertained or if it has a condition precedent. If the unascertained taker becomes ascertained or if the condition precedent is met, the contingent remainder becomes vested.

Keep in mind, though, that a contingent remainder can be contingent *both* because it has a condition precedent and because its taker is unascertained. If only one of these contingencies is resolved, the other remains, and the remainder is still contingent. For example, consider this conveyance:

> *O to A for life, then to A's first child if A*
> *graduated from law school.*

Assume that A does not yet have children and has not graduated from law school. The remainder is contingent *both* because the taker is unascertained and because the conveyance has a condition precedent (graduation from law school). Upon the birth of A's first child, the taker is ascertained, but the condition precedent remains unmet: A still must graduate from law school. Therefore, the remainder is still contingent.

Similarly, if the condition precedent is removed but the taker is still unascertained, the remainder is still contingent. In our prior example, if A graduates from law school but still has no children, the remainder is still contingent even though the condition precedent has been satisfied.

▶ Conveyance of a Fee Tail

As you know, a fee tail in its original form could not be conveyed to another. The fee tail holder (A) could convey only the right to possess the land during A's lifetime. On A's death, the right to possession would pass automatically to A's issue.

However, beginning in the fifteenth century, English courts began to develop ways to convert a fee tail into a fee simple. Eventually, it

---

[32] However, in Chapter 13, we shall see that other doctrines may affect this conveyance.

became well settled that the holder of a fee tail could ***disentail***—that is, convert the fee tail interest into a fee simple—merely by conveying a fee simple.

This is actually as simple and as strange as it sounds. In the following conveyance, assume that O holds in fee tail:

O to A and her heirs.

Simply by purporting to convey a fee simple, O has in fact done so. A now holds a possessory estate in fee simple absolute.

This method of disentailing a fee works only for conveyances made during the grantor's lifetime. The holder of a fee tail cannot disentail by will and certainly not by intestate succession. Therefore, if the holder dies holding a fee tail (that is, without having disentailed during his life-time), then the fee tail passes to the holder's issue, according to the nature of the fee tail estate.

It might seem that this method of disentailing allows the holder to convey a fee simple to another person but does not allow the holder to convert the fee tail to a fee simple and still keep the estate for herself. Not true. The holder of a fee tail can convey to a straw person and have the straw person immediately reconvey to the original holder. The initial conveyance "O to A" conveys to A (the straw person) a fee simple. The straw person can then reconvey this newly disentailed fee to O. O now holds a fee simple.

Since estates held in fee tail are rarely useful in modern times, American jurisdictions have significantly limited fee tail interests. Most prohibit the creation of new fee tail estates and allow holders of existing fee tails to disentail by inter vivos[33] conveyance. In this book, if the directions specify modern law, we will assume that the inter vivos conveyance of a fee tail automatically disentails the fee. The grantee takes a fee simple. However, remember that the holder of a fee tail who wishes to disentail must convey the fee before he or she dies. A fee tail cannot be passed by will or by intestate succession, nor can it be disentailed by will or by intestate succession.

▶ Subsequent Conveyance of a Reversion or a Remainder

A grantor who has retained a reversion can later convey that reversion to another. In that case, the name of the future interest does not change. The new grantee now holds O's reversion. And since a reversion is

---

[33] An inter vivos conveyance is a conveyance made during life, as apposed to a bequest or a devise.

treated as vested (because it is a retained part of O's original estate), the reversion is still treated as vested, even though it is now held by a grantee.

Similarly, a grantee (B) who received a remainder can reconvey that remainder to O. Again, the name of the future interest does not change. O now holds B's remainder. And if the remainder was contingent because of a condition precedent, it is still contingent.

▶ Future Interests Moving into Possession

We have already seen examples of future interests that move into possession. Usually, the name of the estate doesn't change except for no longer being a future interest. For instance, consider the following conveyance:

> *O to A for life, then to B for life, then to C.*

First identify the sate of the title:

> *A has a possessory estate in life estate;*
>
> *B has a vested remainder in life estate;*
>
> *C has a vested remainder in fee simple absolute.*

If A dies, B's life estate moves into possession. Now, the state of the title is this:

> *B has a possessory estate in life estate;*
>
> *C has a vested remainder in fee simple absolute.*

However, sometimes the movement into possession causes additional changes to the names of the estates. For instance, consider the following conveyance:

> *O to A for life, then to B for life,*
> *but if B ever divorces, then to C.*

As always, first identify the state of the title:

> *A has a possessory estate in life estate;*
>
> *B has a vested remainder (subject to divestment) in life estate subject to an executory limitation;*

C has an executory interest in fee simple absolute;

O has a reversion in fee simple absolute.[34]

If A dies and B has not divorced, how does the state of the title change? B now has a possessory estate in life estate, but is it still subject to divestment? Remember that "subject to divestment" applies only to situations in which the interest could be divested *before becoming possessory.* Now B's life estate can never be prevented from becoming possessory. It already *is* possessory. Therefore, B's life estate no longer is subject to divestment. Therefore, here is the state of the title after A dies:

B has a possessory estate in life estate subject to an executory limitation;

C has an executory interest in fee simple absolute;

O has a reversion in fee simple absolute.

▶ Merger

The doctrine of merger allows vested interests to be combined when they come into the hands of the same holder. More specifically:

Merger

If

1. A possessory or vested life estate and the next vested estate in fee simple come into the hands of the same person and

2. These two estates are not separated by another *vested* estate,

Then

3. The life estate merges into the next vested estate held by the same person, and

4. If there is a *contingent* remainder between them, the contingent remainder will be destroyed.
   (*Exception*: If the estates were created in the same document, an intervening contingent estate is safe.)

---

[34] Do you see why O has a reversion? C takes the possessory estate only if B has divorced. Who will take possession if B dies without having divorced?

Here's how merger works. Consider the following conveyance:

O to A for life, then to B.

As you can see, *A has a possessory estate in life estate, and B has a vested remainder in fee simple absolute.* If A later conveys her life estate to B, B will hold both a possessory life estate (pur autre vie) and a vested remainder in fee simple absolute. Since there is no other vested estate between them, these two estates will merge. Now what does B have? When you add B's possessory life estate to B's vested remainder in fee simple absolute, you get a possessory estate in fee simple absolute. In other words, B now holds all possible ownership interests in the property, and the doctrine of merger has combined them into one interest.

The result would be the same if B conveyed his vested remainder to A. Then A would have both the possessory estate in life estate and the vested remainder in fee simple absolute. When you add A's possessory estate in life estate to A's vested remainder in fee simple absolute, you get a possessory estate in fee simple absolute in A.

But what if there were another vested interest in between? Consider this conveyance:

O to A for life, then to B for life, then to C.

As you see, *A has a possessory estate in life estate, B has a vested remainder in life estate, and C has a vested remainder in fee simple absolute.* Now what if A conveys her life estate to C? C would have both the possessory life estate (pur autre vie) and a vested remainder in fee simple absolute. But could these two estates merge? No, because together they do not account for all *vested* interests. B has an intervening vested life estate, which we cannot destroy. Therefore, after A's conveyance to C, the state of the title is this:

C has a possessory estate in life estate pur autre vie;

B has a vested remainder in life estate;

C also has a vested remainder in fee simple absolute.

Now one final example. Consider this conveyance:

O to A for life, then to B for life if B
has reached 21, then to C.
[B is not yet 21.]

As you see, *A has a possessory estate in life estate, B has a* contingent *remainder in life estate, and C has a vested remainder in fee simple absolute.* Now what if A conveys her life estate to C? C would have both the possessory life estate (pur autre vie) and the vested remainder in fee simple absolute. Could these two estates merge? Yes, because the only interest between them is contingent. Their merger destroys B's intervening contingent remainder in life estate. Therefore, after A's conveyance to C, the state of the title is this:

C has a possessory estate in fee simple absolute.

As you can see, the doctrine of merger sometimes allows contingent remainders to be destroyed, therefore making land more **alienable** (saleable). You can imagine that land held in a series of splintered interests would not be very marketable. Who would be willing to pay a good price for a life estate when the measuring life might end any day? And worse yet, who would be willing to pay for a *future* life estate when the measuring life could die before the life estate even became possessory? And how many buyers would be willing to pay for even a *vested* future interest in fee simple absolute if the buyer might have to wait years and years for the prior life estate holders to die?

The only way land held in splintered interests can be easily marketable is if all of the holders of these splintered interests not only agree to sell but also agree on the price, terms, and conditions of the sale and division of the proceeds. Given how common disagreements about such matters are, the odds are not favorable that the land will be marketable any time soon. Therefore, the doctrine of merger does its part to help make land more marketable sooner than it otherwise would be.

As a matter of fact, the doctrine of merger can make for some interesting alliances. Notice that in the prior conveyance A and C could get together and decide to eliminate B's interest. One of them could convey to the other, thus producing a fee simple absolute in one of them. Then the holder of the fee simple absolute could sell the property, and the two of them (A and C) could split the proceeds. This is an unfortunate result for B, but it increases the marketability of land.

▶ The Continuation of Conditions: Destruction of Contingent Remainders

The final post-conveyance factual development we'll consider is this: What happens if a contingent remainder is still contingent when the prior estate ends? Consider this conveyance:

O to A for life, then to B if B reaches 35.

What happens if B has not reached 35 by the time A dies? You might reason that O retains anything O hasn't conveyed and that therefore O must have a reversionary interest that would allow O to take possession of the land until we see if B will reach 35.[35]

However, this result would not have allowed the land to be fully marketable right away. Instead, O would have only a small reversionary interest while waiting for B to either age or die. Certainly, there would be no effective market for such an interest in land. Nor would there be a very healthy market for B's interest, since it was contingent on B's attainment of the age of 35. Since during much of the development of English land law the courts desired to maximize the alienability of land, allowing O to hold the land while waiting for B to turn 35 was not a desirable result.

So, instead, the courts developed a doctrine called the ***destruction of contingent remainders***. According to this doctrine, if a remainder was still contingent when the prior estate ended, the contingent remainder was destroyed, and the right to possession simply moved to the next vested estate.

Doctrine of Destruction of Contingent Remainders

A contingent remainder is destroyed if it is still contingent when the prior estate ends.

Therefore, in our sample conveyance, if A died before B reached 35, B's interest would be destroyed, and the possessory estate would return to O. The state of the title then was this:

O had a possessory estate in fee simple absolute.

You can see that a possessory estate in fee simple absolute is the quintessentially marketable estate. The land was immediately ready for sale. This result was exactly what the courts desired.

The doctrine of destructibility of contingent remainders has been abolished in most American jurisdictions. In jurisdictions that do *not* apply the doctrine of destruction of contingent remainders, the result is exactly what you may have originally predicted: When the prior estate ends and the next interest is a remainder that is still contingent, seisin simply reverts to O while we await the fate of the future interest. If the condition is met, the future interest divests O and becomes possessory. Consider again the conveyance above:

O to A for life, then to B if B reaches 35.

---

[35] In fact, this is exactly how most modern jurisdictions would resolve the situation.

In a jurisdiction that has abolished the destructibility doctrine, if B is 14 when A dies, seisin reverts to O until B either dies or reaches 35. If B dies at 29, seisin remains in O, who then has a possessory estate in fee simple absolute. If B reaches 35, seisin passes to B, who then has a possessory estate in fee simple absolute.

Notice, by the way, that the state of the title would actually change while we are waiting to see if B will reach 35. Immediately after the original conveyance, this is the state of the title:

A has a possessory estate in life estate;

B has a contingent remainder in fee simple absolute;

O has a reversion in fee simple absolute.

But if A dies and B is only 14, possession will *revert* to O, and O's possession will be *interrupted* by B if and when B turns 35. Therefore, while B is aging, the state of the title would be this:

O has a possessory estate in fee simple subject to an executory limitation;

B has a springing executory interest in fee simple absolute.

If and when B reaches 35, the state of the title would be this:

B has a possessory estate in fee simple absolute.

In the rest of the exercises in this book, the directions will tell you whether to apply the doctrine of destructibility of contingent remainders. Apply the Chapter 11 doctrines to the following Study Questions and Practice Exercises. If your Property class did not study merger or destruction of contingent remainders, omit the questions that ask about those doctrines. For the Practice Exercises, you can check the answers in Appendix C to find out which to omit.

▶ Study Questions and Practice Exercises

Practice working with the material in this chapter, and learn it well before you go on to the next chapter. Answer the following questions, using the chart to help you. Make them into flash cards (*including the number of the exercise so you can identify the question later*), add them to your other cards, shuffle, and practice them all again. If you can answer, confidently and without hesitation, the Study Questions and Practice Exercises in Chapters 1-6, you can remove them from your stack. However, it is still a good idea to review them now and then.

11-1 What is the name of the doctrine that combines two or more vested interests when they come into the hands of the same person and are not separated by a vested interest held by someone else?

11-2 What is the name of the doctrine that causes a contingent remainder to fail if its contingencies are not resolved by the time all prior estates have ended?

11-3 In order for the doctrine of merger to combine two vested interests, what two criteria must be met?

11-4 What happens to a contingent remainder that is placed between two vested interests combined by the doctrine of merger?

11-5 If a vested remainder subject to divestment in fee simple subject to executory limitation becomes possessory, what is its new name?

Does the doctrine of merger apply to the following situations? Why or why not?

11-6 O to A for life, then to B for life, then to C. Subsequently C conveys to A.

11-7 O to A for life, then to B if B is then married, otherwise to C. Subsequently C conveys to A. (B is not married.)

11-8 O to A for 10 years, then to B for life if B is then married, then to A.

11-9 O to A for life, then to A's first child for life, then to C. Subsequently C conveys to A. A has no children.

State the title both at the time of the conveyance and after each subsequent factual development:

11-10 O to A for 10 years, then to B for life, then back to O.
O subsequently conveys to C.
C subsequently conveys to B.

11-11 (In this conveyance, be sure to notice all the reasons that the first future interest is contingent.) O to A for life, then to the Mayor of New York City if A has married, but if A never marries, then to B. (A has not yet married.)
Subsequently, A marries.

11-12 O to A for 10 years, then to B.
Subsequently, B dies, devising all her property to C.

11-13 O to A for life, then to B and his heirs, but if B ever allows strip mining on the property, then to C and her heirs.
Subsequently, B dies.

11-14 O to A for life, then to B if B gets married. (B is unmarried.)
Two years later A conveys to O.

11-15 O to A for life, then to A's first child to reach 21.
(A's only child (B) is 17.)
Two years later A dies.

11-16 O to A for 2 years, then to B; however, if B ever uses illegal drugs, then to C.
Two years pass.

11-17 O (who owns in fee tail) to A. (Assume modern law.)
Then A conveys to O.

11-18 O to A for life, then to B's first child and his heirs. (B has no children.)
Subsequently, B and her husband (C) have a child (D), who lives for one hour.
B and C have three more children (E, F, and G).
Then A, B, and C die in a car accident, all without wills.

11-19 O to A for life, then to B, but if B gets divorced, B's interest ends. (B is not divorced.)
Two years later A conveys to O.

The following clients have told you their situations and asked for your advice. Answer their questions.

11-20 "My husband, James, died last month, and I am the executor of his estate. I have to list the estate's assets and file the list with the Probate Court. About 10 years ago, my husband's sister died. A clause in her will said, 'I leave my property at 114 Dalmont Street to my sister Jennifer for life, and then to my brother James for life, and then to my niece Clara.' Do I list this property as one of the estate's assets?"

11-21 "My mother owned a farm in Collier County. She inherited the land from her father, Frank Lange, who farmed it all his life. The deed to her father says, 'To Frank Lange and his heirs so long as he does not cease farming the land.' My mother never farmed the land. She has now died, and I am her only heir. Does someone else have a claim to the land? And if the land is mine, must I farm it?"

11-22 "I hold some land originally bought by my grandfather, and I've always heard that it's something called 'fee tail.' I don't have any children. As a matter of fact, I am the last generation of my family. I want to devise the property to the city so they can make it a park, but someone told me that I can't do that. Is that right?"

11-23 "My grandmother's will gave her home to several people in the family. The will says, 'I give my real estate to my daughter Ruth for life, then to my brother John's son Keith for life if Keith has reached 50, then to my granddaughter, Elaine.' I am Elaine, and Ruth is my mother. Keith has developed a gambling addiction, and my mother and I don't want him to lose his life estate to his creditors. Is there anything we can do to prevent that?"

More Efforts to Further Alienability

In Chapter 11, we worked with some concepts and doctrines that come into play only according to factual developments occurring *after* the original conveyance. You will need to apply those concepts and doctrines only if you are given an original conveyance *and* some subsequent factual developments.

The doctrines in this chapter, however, do their work *immediately when the conveyance is created*. They will apply, if at all, to the original conveyance the moment it is created. Like the doctrines of merger and destructibility of contingent remainders, both of the following doctrines have the effect of promoting alienability. They were developed to help keep land as marketable as possible by reducing the number of splintered ownership interests.

Some Property classes do not have time to cover these doctrines. If your course will omit either or both of these doctrines, simply skip the section(s) pertaining to the doctrine(s). The answers for the Study Questions and Practice Exercises in Appendix C will identify which doctrines are relevant to which questions so you can tell which questions to skip.

▶ The Rule in Shelley's Case

The Rule in Shelley's Case prevents a grantor from using the same document to convey a life estate to a grantee and a remainder to *that grantee's heirs*. If the grantor attempts this conveyance, the remainder to the grantee's heirs is read instead as a remainder to the grantee. Here is an example:

O to A for life, then to ~~A's heirs~~ <u>A</u>.

The Rule in Shelley's Case essentially strikes out the words "A's heirs" and substitutes "A." The state of the title is this:

> *A has a possessory estate in life estate;*
>
> *A also has a vested remainder in fee simple absolute.*

The Rule is limited in several important ways. First, it applies only to remainders, not to executory interests. For instance, consider this conveyance:

O to A for life, <u>then to A's heirs at the</u>
<u>*conclusion of A's funeral*</u>.

Since the Rule does not apply to executory interests, the interest conveyed to A's heirs is safe. The state of the title is this:

> *A has a possessory estate in life estate;*
>
> *O has a reversion in fee simple subject to an executory limitation;*
>
> *A's heirs have a springing executory interest.*

Second, the Rule applies only when the grantor conveyed both interests in the same document. For instance, if O conveyed a life estate to A (reserving a reversion) and subsequently conveyed the reversion to A's heirs, the Rule would not apply. Similarly, if O conveyed a life estate to A and a remainder to B and subsequently B conveyed to A's heirs, the Rule would not apply.

Third, the Rule applies only to conveyances "to [the grantee's] heirs."[36] It does not apply, for instance, to conveyances "to [the grantee's] children" or "to [the grantee's] issue" or to conveyances to named persons who are likely to become the grantee's heirs.

Finally, the Rule in Shelley's Case applies only if the estates are both legal or both equitable. In this context, an equitable interest is an interest of the beneficiary by a trust. A legal interest is an interest that is not an equitable interest, either because the property is not the subject of a trust at all or because we are referring to the ownership interest of the trustee rather than to the ownership interest of the beneficiary. In this book, we will assume that all interests are legal, so we will not concern ourselves with this exception.

In most jurisdictions, the Rule in Shelley's Case has been abrogated and thus does not limit new conveyances, but older conveyances will still require application of the Rule for some time.

---

[36] Or "the heirs of the grantee's body."

Rule in Shelley's Case

If

1. The same document

2. Conveys a life estate to a grantee and

3. A remainder to *that grantee's* heirs,

Then

4. The conveyance to the grantee's heirs is read as a conveyance to the grantee.

▶ Shelley's Case and Merger

Notice the result of the application of the Rule in Shelley's Case in our first example above. The conveyance was

O to A for life, then to ~~A's heirs~~ A̲.

After the application of the Rule in Shelley's Case, the state of the title is this:

> *A has a possessory estate in life estate;*

> *A also has a vested remainder in fee simple absolute.*

What do you suppose might happen then? You've probably already guessed that the doctrine of merger[37] would combine these two interests. The state of the title would then be this:

> *A has a possessory estate in fee simple absolute.*

Of course, as you recall from our discussion of merger in Chapter 11, an intervening vested estate will prevent merger. Therefore, merger would not apply in our second example above:

O to A for life, then to B for life, then to ~~A's heirs~~ A̲.

B's intervening vested remainder in life estate would prevent A's two estates from merging. After the application of the Rule in Shelley's Case, the state of the title would be this:

> *A has a possessory estate in life estate;*

---

[37] See Chapter 11.

B has a vested remainder in life estate;

A also has a vested remainder in fee simple absolute.

Rule in Shelley's Case and Merger

1. *0 to A for life, then to A's heirs.*

   The Rule in Shelley's Case reads the contingent remainder in A's heirs as a remainder in A.

   Is the remainder still contingent? No, because now the holder of the remainder is ascertained, so the remainder is vested.

   Does merger apply? Yes, because the remainder is now vested. The merger doctrine merges the life estate into the vested remainder.

2. *0 to A for life, then to A's heirs if A survives B.*

   The Rule in Shelley's Case converts the contingent remainder in A's heirs into a remainder in A.

   Is the remainder in A still contingent? Yes. The holder is now ascertained, but the condition precedent remains.

   Does merger apply? No, because the remainder is contingent.

3. *0 to A for life, then to B for life, then to A's heirs.*

   The Rule in Shelley's Case converts the contingent remainder in A's heirs into a remainder in A.

   Is the remainder in A still contingent? No. Now, the holder of the remainder is ascertained. The remainder is now vested.

   Does merger apply? No, because there is an intervening vested estate (B's life estate).

▶ The Doctrine of Worthier Title

As we just saw, the Rule in Shelley's Case prevents a grantor from conveying a possessory estate to a grantee and a future interest to that grantee's heirs. The doctrine of worthier title impedes the grantor in a slightly different way. It prevents a grantor from conveying a life estate to a grantee and a future interest (a remainder or an executory interest) to the *grantor's* heirs. The doctrine was developed, in part, to further alienability. After all, an interest held by O's heirs was not alienable at all during O's lifetime because O's heirs are not ascertained until O dies. Also, holding land by virtue of an inheritance was thought to be "worthier" than holding land as a result of an **inter vivos** conveyance (a conveyance made during the grantor's lifetime).[38]

If the grantor attempts such an inter vivos conveyance, the future interest to the grantor's heirs is read instead as a reversionary interest to the *grantor*. Here is an example:

O to A for life, then to ~~O's heirs~~ O̲.

The doctrine of worthier title essentially strikes the words "O's heirs," substituting "O" in their place. The state of the title is this:

A has a possessory estate in life estate;

O has a reversion in fee simple absolute.

The doctrine can apply both to attempted remainders and to attempted executory interests. For instance:

O to A for life, then to B, but if B uses the land for a tavern, then to ~~O's heirs~~ O̲.

The state of the title is this:

A has a possessory estate in life estate;

B has a vested remainder in fee simple subject to a condition subsequent;

O has a right of entry in fee simple absolute.

Just as we saw with the Rule in Shelley's Case, the doctrine of worthier title applies only to conveyances "to [the grantor's] heirs."[39] It does not apply, for instance, to conveyances "to [the grantor's] children" or "to [the grantor's] issue" or to conveyances to named persons who are likely to become the grantor's heirs.

The American version of the doctrine of worthier title has been treated as only a *presumption* that the grantor intended to retain a reversion. The presumption can be rebutted by contrary evidence.

---

[38] Also, like several other future interests doctrines, the doctrine of worthier title discouraged landowners from trying to avoid the feudal equivalent of property taxes due when land passed by inheritance.

[39] Or "the heirs of the grantor's body."

> **Doctrine of Worthier Title**
>
> **If**
>
> **1.** The same intervivos conveyance
>
> **2.** Conveys an inherently limited estate to a grantee and
>
> **3.** A remainder or an executory interest to *the grantor's* heirs,
>
> **Then**
>
> The conveyance to the grantor's heirs is read as a conveyance to the grantor.

▶ Worthier Title and Merger

Just as we saw with the Rule in Shelley's Case, the doctrine of merger can apply in concert with the doctrine of worthier title. For instance, consider this conveyance:

> ***O to A for life, then one day
> later to O's heirs.***

Notice that this conveyance creates a gap between A's life estate and the interest the grantor attempts to give to O's heirs. Therefore, without applying any doctrines, the state of the title is this:

A has a possessory estate in life estate;

O has a reversion in fee simple subject to an executory limitation;

O's heirs have a springing executory interest.

However, since the doctrine of worthier title applies to executory interests, we strike the words "O's heirs" and replace them with "O." Now, A has a possessory estate in life estate, and O has all remaining interests. Merger operates to combine O's interests into a reversion in fee simple absolute.

REVIEW

Rule in Shelley's Case

O to A for life, then to ~~A's heirs~~ A.

1. The same intervivos conveyance
2. Conveys an inherently limited estate to a grantee and
3. A remainder to *that grantee's* heirs

Doctrine of Worthier Title

O to A for life, then to ~~O's heirs~~ O.

1. The same document
2. Conveys an inherently limited estate to a grantee and
3. A remainder or an executory interest to *the grantor's* heirs

Destructibility of Contingent Remainders (from Chapter 11)

O to A for life, ~~then to B if B is 21~~.

[A dies before B reaches 21.]

A remainder is destroyed if it does not vest at or before the termination of the preceding estate. The doctrine does not apply to executory interests.

Merger

O to A for life, then to B.

[Then A conveys to B.] B now has a possessory estate in the fee simple.

If

1. A possessory or vested life estate and the next vested estate in fee simple come into the hands of the same person and
2. These two estates are not separated by another *vested* estate,

Then

3. The estates merge, and
4. Any *contingent* remainder between them is destroyed.

(*Exception*: If the estates were created in the same document, an intervening contingent estate is safe.)

▶ Study Questions and Practice Exercises

Practice working with the material in this chapter, and learn it well before you go on to the next chapter. Answer the following questions, using the chart to help you. Make them into flash cards (*including the number of the exercise so you can identify the question later*), add them to your other cards, shuffle, and practice them all again.

If your Property class did not study one of the doctrines covered in this chapter, you can identify which of these practice exercises to omit by referring to the answers in Appendix C.

For each of the following conveyances, give the state of the title.

12-1 *O to A for life, then to A's heirs and their heirs.*

12-2 *O to A for life, then to B for life, then to A's heirs and their heirs.*

12-3 *O to A for life, then to O's heirs and their heirs.*

12-4 *O to A for life, then to B for life, then to O's heirs and their heirs.*

12-5 *O to A for life, then to A's children.* (A has two children, B and C.)

12-6 *O to A for life, but if A divorces, then to O's heirs.*

12-7 *O to A for life, then to B.* Then B conveys to A's heirs.

12-8 *O to A for life, then to B for life, then to B's heirs and their heirs.*

12-9 *O to A for life, and 2 years later to O's heirs.*

12-10 *O to A for life, then to B.* Then B conveys to O's heirs.

The Infamous Rule Against Perpetuities

13

No interest is good unless it must vest [and close], if at all, not later than twenty-one years after some life in being at the creation of the interest.

—John C. Gray

The Rule Against Perpetuities is the final doctrine in our study of methods for furthering alienability. The Rule has a reputation for being difficult to understand and for tripping up law students and lawyers alike,[40] but if you take it step by step, you'll find that the Rule is not as difficult as its reputation might cause you to believe.

Like the doctrines in Chapter 12, the Rule Against Perpetuities does its work *immediately when the conveyance is created*. It will apply, if at all, to the conveyance the moment it is created. We will begin our study of the Rule in a moment, but before we do, you'll need to be sure you remember a couple of concepts from earlier chapters. Also, our exploration of the Rule will go smoother if you meet a few miscellaneous characters first.

▶ Preparing to Study the Rule

▶ Vested Interests vs. Contingent Interests

First, remember the difference between a vested interest and a contingent interest. A contingent interest is a future interest that may or may not ever become possessory. It has one (or both) of these two characteristics:

---

[40] For a cinematic example of a lawyer who was caught by the Rule not once but twice, see the movie *Body Heat*, starring Kathleen Turner and William Hurt.

Contingent Interest

1. The identity of the holder is unascertained, or
2. The interest is subject to a condition precedent (other than the termination of the prior estate).

Conversely, a vested interest is a future interest that already has the right to become possessory. A vested interest has both of the following characteristics:

Vested Interest

1. The holder is ascertained, and
2. The interest is *not* subject to a condition precedent (other than the termination of the prior estate).

Previously, we have spoken only of remainders as "vested" or "contingent," but in this chapter, we'll be applying these terms and the concepts they describe to executory interests as well. You do not need to add the term "vested" or "contingent" to the *name* of the executory interest when you are identifying the state of the title—just be ready to apply the concepts of vesting to executory interests as well as to remainders.

▶ Closed Interests vs. Interests Subject to Open

Remember the difference between a closed interest and an interest subject to open. An interest is subject to open if it is given to a class of people and if that class could grow. For instance, an interest given to A's children is subject to open as long as A is alive and therefore could have more children.[41] Conversely, an interest given to A's children is closed if A is dead and therefore can have no more children.

---

[41] For the purposes of Property law, any living person is considered fertile.

The Three Vulnerable Future Interests

Contingent remainders

Vested remainders subject to open

Executory interests

▶ When a Will Is Effective

No conveyance occurs when a testator first executes his or her will. A will does not become effective until the testator dies. You will be applying the Rule Against Perpetuities to conveyances the moment they are created, so you will be applying the Rule to testamentary conveyances at the moment of the testator's death, not earlier.

▶ The Fetus (Gestation) Rule

A child is considered alive (that is, considered a life in being) from the time the child is conceived *if the child is later born alive*.

▶ Medical Advances in Treating Infertility

Recent years have seen medical advancements such as in vitro fertilization, surrogate motherhood, and sperm storage. These advancements did not exist when the common law of the Rule Against Perpetuities developed. For purposes of our analysis of the Rule, ignore them.[42]

▶ The Fertile Octogenarian

For the purposes of Property law, any person who is alive is considered capable of having more children, no matter the age or physical condition of the person.

---

[42] Some states have enacted statutes to deal with the Property law implications of some of these medical advancements.

► The Unborn Widow

Just as no living person has heirs or devisees, no living person has a widow or a widower. We already know that when a conveyance uses descriptive terms such as these, the identities of the holders usually are unascertained. For purposes of our study of the Rule Against Perpetuities, we'll need to remember something else about these terms: The persons who ultimately meet these descriptions might not be alive at the time of the conveyance. For instance, consider this conveyance:

O to A for life, then to O's widow.

It is possible that the person to whom O will be married at the time of his death could be a person not presently alive. This scenario is possible even if O is presently married to B. For example, assume that O is 25 years old. A year after the conveyance, X is born. A could live 30 more years. During that time, O and B could divorce or B could die. A year before A dies, O (then 54 years old) could marry X (now 28). Thus, O's widow could be a person who was not alive at the time of the conveyance.

You may well be wondering why we care whether O's widow (or heir or devisee) might not have been born at the time of the conveyance. As we shall soon see, the Rule Against Perpetuities makes this question vital.

Now, we're ready to explore the Rule itself. We'll start with the purpose of the Rule so its strange terms will not seem so puzzling or arbitrary.

► The Rule's Purpose

Having inherited or acquired large holdings, wealthy English landholders desired to keep those holdings safely in the family forever, or at least as close to forever as they could achieve. They also wanted to control the actions of their family members long into the future. Creative use of many of the estates and limitations we've studied allowed landholders to prevent the sale of family holdings and to control family members well after the holder's death. The courts and the crown tried a number of methods for freeing land (and people) from this dead-hand control. The capstone of these methods was the Rule Against Perpetuities.

Try thinking of the Rule as an agreement between a grantor and the rest of his community. Imagine that a grantor wants to create a contingent future interest—an interest that might or might not ever vest. Maybe the grantor wants to condition vesting on the happening of some event—something that might or might not ever happen, like this:

O to A, but if the land ever ceases to be used for a farm, then to B.

In this conveyance, B might or might not ever take possession, depending on how the land is used. Yet B's contingent interest will hang around, clouding the title and impairing conveyances and other profitable use of the land forever.

Now, imagine that we are the other people in the grantor's community. Many of us are landowners, too, and we are sympathetic to the idea that landowners want to be free to dispose of their property as they please. But we are also concerned about the effect of unlimited contingent interests. Contingent future interests tie up land for many, many years and prevent people from doing good things with that land. They prevent people from developing the land or selling it to others who want to develop it. They prohibit uses that would be good for the rest of the community. They effectively prohibit people from being able to use the land as collateral for a loan. They discourage the owners of the splintered interests from improving the land or even from maintaining it very well. For instance, consider our example above:

O to A, but if the land ever ceases to be used for a farm, then to B.

Most likely, B could not sell her interest in the land, for who would buy an interest that might never come into possession? And what bank would lend money to B using her interest in the land as collateral? And what if years later the city of Chicago had grown up all around the land, but A's heirs had to continue to farm the land or else lose it to B's heirs? These results aren't good for anybody.

We don't mind vested future interests so much—interests that are certain to become possessory eventually. People may be more willing to buy them, banks are more willing to lend money on them, the holders are better able to get together with each other to sell a fee simple, and the holders are more likely to see that the land is well maintained if they're sure that the land will one day be theirs. For example, here is a vested future interest:

O to A for life, then to B.

Both A and B can probably sell their interests, use their interests as collateral for loans, or cooperate to sell a fee simple. They may be more likely to take good care of the land. They are more likely to agree on development plans. Vested future interests are far more flexible than contingent future interests.

Since we, the community, make the laws and since contingent future interests cause such problems, we are considering outlawing them entirely. We don't much mind vested future interests, but contingent future interests have become a problematic, and despite our reluctance to impinge on the rights of property owners, we're inclined to outlaw contingent interests.

The grantor knows what we think about the difficulties caused by contingent future interests, so the grantor comes to us to ask permission to create a contingent interest. He says, "I know you don't like having contingent interests hanging around for a long time. Can't we compromise? Please just agree to let this future interest be contingent for the rest of all our lives plus 21 years. That way, I'm only controlling the land for our lifetimes plus the childhood of the firstborn of the next generation. After that future person (someone born just after we all die) has had a chance to reach 21, that person will be old enough to manage the land. I'm willing to give up trying to control the land longer than that."

This seems like a good compromise. It allows us to maintain an owner's right to control the land for a while after the owner's death, but we can at least be assured that this control won't go on forever. We'll agree to let this interest be contingent for that long, *but only if we can be absolutely sure that by the end of that time it will have either vested and closed or failed (and therefore ended)*. The time period the grantor has proposed is a very long time. We're not willing to wait *at all* unless the grantor can prove to us that at the end of that time the interest will either be vested and closed or be eliminated (because it has failed). It's OK with us if the interest is still a *future* interest. It doesn't have to be possessory already. But we've got to be absolutely sure that by the end of that time either it's vested and closed or it's gone.

The grantor agrees to abide by our concession and creates the contingent future interest. Now comes your job. You must make sure that the grantor has kept his end of the bargain. You have to check to be sure that this contingent future interest will stop being contingent within the period we agreed to. It can stop being contingent *either* by becoming vested and closed *or* by failing. Either possibility is OK with us. But we've got to be sure that it will do one or the other within our lifetimes plus 21 years. If not, we will *strike out the offending interest*. We will strike it out *immediately, at the time the grantor makes the conveyance*.

So here's a statement of the rule we've made:

Rule Against Perpetuities

A future interest is void *the moment it's created* if

1. It is in a *grantee* (a remainder or an executory interest);

2. It is either *contingent* (given to an unascertained taker or subject to a condition precedent or both) or *subject to open*; and

3. It might still exist and *still be contingent or subject to open* longer than 21 years after the death of the last person alive at the time of the conveyance.

▶ The Rule's Meaning

The Rule Against Perpetuities describes a time period during which contingent or open future interests are permitted. To understand the Rule, you'll need to understand how to handle two analytical tasks: (1) calculating the permitted time period and (2) deciding how long an interest might remain contingent or open.

▶ Calculating the Permitted Time Period

Rather than describing the permitted time period using a number (for example, 70 years or 90 years or 100 years), the original version of the Rule paints a word picture of the permitted time period. The Rule defines the time period as 21 years after the death of the last **life in being** (the last person alive at the time of the conveyance). Consider the following conveyance:

O to A for life, then to A's children.

Assume that we can look into the future and see that A will be the last life in being to die and that A will live 50 more years. The time period for our analysis would be 71 years.

You may have already anticipated a problem with the Rule's approach. We must test the conveyance immediately upon its creation. Therefore, it is then that we must apply the Rule. But at the time of the conveyance, we cannot know when the last living person will die. Therefore, we must be prepared to account for all possible life spans for the lives in being. Luckily, once you become familiar with how the Rule works, this will not turn out to be as much of a problem as it may initially appear.

▶ Deciding How Long an Interest Might Remain Contingent

Here is where the Rule gets interesting. Remember that the Rule will cause the contingent or open interest to fail at its *creation* if we cannot be sure that its life span won't exceed the permitted time period. The question is not whether the interest might vest and close within the time period, but whether there is *any possibility that it might not*.

Remember also that your job is not to try to *save* the contingent or open interest. Your job is to *test* it. If you can conceive of any possible scenario in which the interest might still be contingent or open after the time period expires, then the Rule has been violated. Consequently, you must imagine all possible story lines. You are trying to find a story line in which the interest violates the Rule. If no such story line is possible, then the interest passes your test.

Again, consider our previous conveyance and assume that A has no children:

O to A for life, then to A's children.

The vulnerable interest is the contingent remainder given to A's children. Since A has no children at present, the remainder has no ascertained holder. Here is the question: What is the longest possible time it might take before we'll either have an ascertained holder or know for sure that there will never be an ascertained holder? In other words, what is the last possible time for A to have a child? Answer: Any children of A's will be conceived by the time A dies.

Now we know the longest period of time that the remainder might remain contingent. It will either vest or fail at A's death. The next step is to compare that *possible* life span to the *permitted* life span.

Recall that the permitted life span is 21 years after the death of the last person who was alive at the time of the conveyance. A was alive at the time of the conveyance, so A is a life in being. According to the Rule, when A dies, the contingent remainder could remain contingent for 21 more years. But we just decided that the last possible time for A to conceive a child (and therefore either satisfy or fail to satisfy the contingency) is immediately prior to A's death. So the contingent remainder passes our test.[43] It cannot possibly remain contingent longer than A's lifetime.

Consider the same conveyance, but this time assume that A has two children (B and C):

O to A for life, then to A's children.

B and C have a vested remainder, but since A is still alive, the remainder is subject to open. Therefore, the remainder is vulnerable to the Rule, and we must test it.

Again, remember the question: What is the longest possible time it might take before the vested remainder will close? In other words, what is the last possible time for A to have another child? The answer is the same: Any children of A's will be conceived by the time A dies. Therefore, the remainder will close at A's death.

Again, the next step is to compare that possible life span to the permitted life span. The permitted life span is 21 years after the death of the last person who was alive at the time of the conveyance. A was alive at the time of the conveyance, so A is a life in being. According to the Rule,

---

[43] Assuming that it will also close within the permitted time period. It will, as the discussion will next demonstrate.

when A dies, the remainder could remain open for 21 more years, but it won't need that long. As we just decided, the last possible time for A to conceive a child is immediately prior to A's death. So the open remainder passes our test. It cannot possibly remain open longer than A's lifetime.

One final reminder: Being able to prove that an interest will *fail* within the permitted time period is just as good as being able to prove that it will vest. The interest violates the Rule *only* if its fate might still be undecided at the end of the permitted time period.

▶ Validating Life

What we just did was to find a ***validating life***. A validating life is someone whose life proves that the interest will either fail or vest and close within the permitted time period. In our example above, A is the validating life. A is the person who will determine whether and when the remainder will either fail or both vest and close. Since A is a life in being and since the interest will either fail or vest and close immediately upon A's death, the interest passes our test. It does not violate the Rule Against Perpetuities.

▶ An Example of an Interest That Violates the Rule

Let's look at the same conveyance now, but make one small change. Consider this conveyance:

O to A for life, then to A's children who reach 30.

[B and C are 32 and 30, respectively.]

B and C have a vested remainder, but since A is still alive, the remainder is subject to open. Therefore, the remainder is vulnerable to the Rule, and we must test it.

Again, remember the question: What is the longest possible time it might take before the vested remainder will close? In this conveyance, only A's children who reach 30 can be a part of the class. So this remainder might not close on A's death. If A has another child (D) and then dies immediately, we won't yet know whether D will reach 30. If D reaches 30, D would be added to the class, but it would take us 30 years to find out.

Compare *that* time period (*30* years after the deaths of A and everyone else alive now) to the *permitted* time period (*21* years after the deaths of everyone alive now). The remainder could remain open longer than the permitted time period. Therefore, neither A nor any other person can prove to us that all of the class members will be identified by 21 years after the time A (and everyone else alive now) dies. There is no validating life, and the remainder violates the Rule Against Perpetuities.

▶ A Step-by-Step Approach for Applying the Rule

Here's a procedure to follow when you're checking an interest. The procedure takes you through every small conceptual step. After you have become comfortable with the Rule and the way it works, you will be able to skip a number of these steps, but for now, these steps will keep you from making conceptual mistakes. As we describe each step, we'll analyze a sample conveyance. We'll start with this conveyance:

O to A for life, then to B for life, then to O's widow.

Step 1: Draw vertical lines to separate the different interests, as we have done throughout this book. Then identify the state of the title according to the conveyance.

O to A for life, | then to B for life, | then to O's widow.

A has a possessory estate in life estate;

B has a vested remainder in life estate;

O's widow has a contingent remainder in fee simple absolute;

O has a reversion in fee simple absolute.

Step 2: Look for any future interests in a *grantee*. You're looking *below* the line for remainders or executory interests. You're not concerned about any future interests in the grantor (those above the line) because, as you recall, the grantor's retained interests are always deemed vested.[44] Here we find two such interests:

B's vested remainder in life estate;

O's widow's contingent remainder in fee simple absolute.

---

[44] Some states have controlled the duration of possibilities of reverter and rights of entry by enacting separate statutes to limit those grantor interests.

Step 3: If you find any future interests in a grantee, check each one to see if it is both vested and closed. If the interest is already vested and closed, it is not vulnerable to the Rule. If it is either contingent or subject to open, it's vulnerable. If you have found any contingent or open future interests in a grantee, underline them.

O to A for life, | then to B for life,
| <u>then to O's widow</u>.

Step 4: For each contingent or open future interest in a grantee, identify the necessary factual developments for vesting and closing, and write them beside the conveyance.

O's widow:

> *The holder must be ascertained, so the event that will vest the interest (or cause it to fail) is <u>O's death</u>.*

Step 5: Now circle all of the lives in being (the people alive at the time of the conveyance).

O, A, and B. (We cannot say that O's widow is alive because we don't know who she will be.)

Step 6: Now consider the first vulnerable interest you have found. See if it might *still* be contingent or open longer than the lifetimes of everyone you circled plus 21 years. You are looking for a validating life. The validating life will probably be someone you circled. Can one of the people you circled prove to you that the interest is certain to *either* vest and close *or* fail within that time? If so, the interest survives the Rule Against Perpetuities. If not, it fails.

O's widow:

> *On O's death, we'll know the fate of this remainder. One of two things will happen: <u>Either</u> O will have a widow and we'll know who she is (thus, the remainder will be vested), <u>or</u> O will die unmarried and the remainder will fail at that moment.*
>
> *O is the validating life. O was alive at the time of the conveyance (one of the people you circled), and the remainder to O's widow will either vest or fail at the moment of O's death. The remainder to O's widow survives the Rule.*

Now we are going to switch examples so we can see an example of an interest that violates the Rule. Consider this conveyance:

> ***O to A for life, then to A's first child
> if he or she reaches 25.***

[A currently has no children.]

Applying step 1, we find

> ***O to A for life,*** | ***then to A's first child
> if he or she reaches 25.*** |

A has a possessory estate in life estate;

A's first child has a contingent remainder in fee simple absolute;

O has a reversion in fee simple absolute.

The interest that is vulnerable to the Rule (steps 2 and 3) is *A's first child's contingent remainder.* In step 4, we see that the remainder is contingent for two reasons: The holder is unascertained, and the remainder has a condition precedent (reaching 25). Therefore, to vest the remainder, *A must have a child and that child must reach 25.* In step 5, we circle the lives in being: O and A.

Step 6: *There is no validating life. Neither O nor anyone else can prove to us that we'll know the fate of the remainder in time. True, A's first child (if any) will be ascertained upon O's death. So far so good. But that child still must reach 25. We'll still have to wait 25 years to find out whether the child will meet the condition precedent. But the Rule requires us to be sure that we'll know within 21 years of the death of the last remaining life in being, not 25 years. Therefore, the interest violates the Rule.* Now we must go on to step 7.

Step 7: If the contingent interest violates the Rule, strike the whole interest (all the words between the vertical lines you drew). Now revise your classification of the title.

> ***O to A for life,*** | ~~***then to A's first child if
> he or she reaches 25.***~~ |

A has a possessory estate in life estate;

O has a reversion in fee simple absolute.

Step 8: If there is *another* contingent or open interest in a grantee, repeat this procedure.

A Step-by-Step Approach for Applying the Rule

Step 1: Draw vertical lines to separate the different interests. Then identify the state of the title according to the conveyance.

Step 2: Look for any future interests in a *grantee*.

Step 3: If you find any future interests in a grantee, check each one to see if it is contingent or open. If so, it's vulnerable. Underline it.

Step 4: Identify the necessary factual developments for vesting and closing, and write them beside the conveyance.

Step 5: Circle all of the lives in being.

Step 6: See if the interest might *still* be contingent or open longer than the lifetimes of everyone you circled plus 21 years. Look for a validating life.

Step 7: If the contingent interest violates the Rule, strike the whole interest, and revise your classification of the title.

Step 8: If there is *another* contingent or open interest in a grantee, repeat this procedure.

In the next chapter, we'll go through some examples to see how the Rule works and to practice analyzing conveyances. First, however, the following Study Questions will help to reinforce some of the material in this chapter.

▶ Study Questions

Answer the following questions. Make them into flash cards (*including the number of the exercise so you can identify the question later*), add them to your other cards, shuffle, and practice them all again.

13-1 State from memory the Rule Against Perpetuities as described by John Gray and modified on page 135.

13-2 Does the Rule Against Perpetuities operate immediately at the time the conveyance is attempted or later?

13-3 Is the Rule Against Perpetuities applicable to future interests in the grantor, future interests in a grantee, or both?

13-4 Name the future interests that are vulnerable to the Rule Against Perpetuities.

13-5 When does a conveyance made in a will operate?

13-6 What is a "life in being"?

13-7 If a child has been conceived but not born at the time of the conveyance, is that child considered a life in being?

13-8 When does the holder of a conveyance to D's widow, widower, heir, or devisee become ascertained?

13-9 What is wrong with the following sentence:
The Rule Against Perpetuities requires that to be valid a contingent interest must be certain to vest and close within 21 years after the death of the last life in being at the time of the conveyance.

13-10 What is wrong with the following sentence:
If a contingent interest might vest and close within 21 years after the death of the last life in being, the interest does not violate the Rule Against Perpetuities.

13-11 How long is the permitted time period created by the Rule Against Perpetuities?

13-12 What is a validating life?

Now for more practice in applying the Rule. You will need to read the words of the conveyance carefully, apply them precisely, and avoid making assumptions about probabilities. Remember, we're interested in certainties.

▶ Danger Signs

Some characteristics increase the odds that a conveyance violates the Rule. Take note of the following danger signs.

RAP Danger Signs

1. The condition is not personal to someone.

2. There is an identified age or time period of more than 21 years.

3. An interest is given to a generation after the next generation (for example, to grandchildren).

4. A conveyance requires that a holder survive someone who is merely described rather than named.

5. An identified event that would normally happen well within 21 years, but might not.

6. The holder won't be identified until the death of someone merely described rather than named.

► Examples

► 1. The condition is not personal to someone.

Step 1:

O to A for life, | then to B, | but if the land is ever used for a tavern, then to C. |

A has a possessory estate in life estate;

B has a vested remainder in fee simple subject to an executory limitation;

C has an executory interest in fee simple absolute.

Steps 2 & 3: B has a remainder, but it's already vested and closed. Therefore, B's interest does not violate the Rule. C's executory interest, however, is *not* vested. It is suject to a condition precedent.

Step 4: For C's executory interest to vest, the land would have to be used for a tavern.

Step 5: Lives in being: O, A, B, and C.

Step 6: C's executory interest would vest any time any future holder of B's interest used the land for a tavern. That could be hundreds of years from now. There is no validating life. The conveyance violates the Rule.

However, notice that the executory interest would have survived if the triggering condition had identified by name the person who must not use the land for a tavern, like so: "but if B ever uses the land for a tavern, then to C." In that case, the triggering event will happen, if at all, during a life in being (B). The executory interest would not violate the Rule.

► 2. There is an identified age or time period of more than 21 years.

Step 1:

O to A for life, | then to A's children who reach 25. |

[A has one child, B, who is 25.]

A has a possessory estate in life estate;

B has a vested remainder in fee simple subject to open.

Steps 2 & 3: B's remainder is already vested, but it is subject to open.

Step 4: To qualify, a new child of A's would have to reach 25.

Step 5: Lives in being: O, A, and B.

Step 6: Consider this scenario: One day after the conveyance, A has another child (C). The next day A and everyone else except this new child, C, die. Is it possible that C might reach 25 (and therefore qualify for the future interest)? Yes. How long would it take? 25 years. Thus, B's remainder might not close within 21 years after the death of the last person alive right now. There is no validating life who can ensure that this interest will close in time. Therefore, B's remainder is void.[45]

However, notice that the remainder would have survived if the triggering condition had been limited to reaching 21. In that case, the triggering event would happen, if at all, by 21 years after the death of a life in being (A). The remainder would survive the Rule.

▶ **3. An interest is given to a generation after the next generation.**

Step 1:

O to A for life, | then to A's grandchildren. |
[A has one child (B) and one grandchild (C).]

A has a possessory estate in life estate;

C has a vested remainder in fee simple subject to open.

Steps 2 & 3: C's remainder is already vested, but it is subject to open.

Step 4: A and all children of A would have to die before all of A's grandchildren would be identified.

Step 5: Lives in being: O, A, B, and C.

Step 6: Consider this scenario: One day after the conveyance, A has another child (X). The next day A, B, and O die. Is it possible that X might have a child someday, thus creating a new grandchild for X? Yes. And is it possible that it would take X more than 21 years to have that child? Definitely. Thus, C's remainder might not close within 21 years after the death of the last person alive right now. There is no validating life that can ensure that this interest will close in time. Therefore, C's remainder is void.

---

[45] This and other descriptions in this chapter incorporate aspects of the "Create, Kill, and Count" approach developed by Professors Charles Nelson and Peter Wendel in their book, *A Possessory Estates and Future Primer* (West Publishing Co., 1996).

However, notice that the remainder would have survived if the conveyance had been to A's children rather than to A's grandchildren. In that case, all of A's children would have been identified by the time A died. The remainder would close immediately upon the death of A (a life in being). The remainder would survive the Rule.

Notice also that the remainder would have survived if the conveyance had been made in O's will. In that case, all of A's children would have already been conceived or born by the time of the conveyance, so all of A's grandchildren would be identified by the time the last of A's children died. Since all of A's children would be lives in being, the class would close immediately upon the death of the last life in being.

▶ **4. A conveyance requires that a holder survive someone who is merely described rather than named (the "unborn widow").**

Step 1:

> ### *O to A for life, | then to A's widow for life, | then to A's children then living. |*

> [A is presently married to B and has one child (C).]

A has a possessory estate in life estate;

A's widow has a contingent remainder in life estate;

A's children then living have a contingent remainder in fee simple absolute.

Steps 2 & 3: Both remainders are contingent.

Step 4: A's widow's remainder will be vested as soon as she is ascertained, which will happen immediately upon A's death.

The remainder to A's children who survive his widow will be vested as soon as the takers are ascertained and the condition precedent is met, which will happen upon the death of A's widow.

Step 5: Lives in being: O, A, B, and C.

Step 6: The remainder to A's widow is valid because it will either vest or fail immediately upon A's death, and A is a life in being. A's widow (either B or someone else) will be ascertained at the time A dies.

However, the remainder to A's children "then living" is a different matter. A might not be married to B when he dies. He might be married to someone who is not yet born (X) and who therefore is not a life in being.[47] Also, since A is alive, A might have another child (Y), who would not be a life in being either. So here's the troublesome scenario:

Immediately after the conveyance, X is born. She grows up. During that time, B dies. A meets X and marries her. They have another child (Y), who also is not a life in being. Then A, C, and all other people alive at the time of the original conveyance die, at which point the 21-year clock begins to tick. A's widow (X) and A's afterborn child (Y) are still alive, but the clock is ticking. For the remainder to "A's children then living" to vest, Y must outlive X. What if X lives more than 21 years after A and everyone else died? The 21-year clock would strike, and we still wouldn't know whether Y would outlive X. Therefore, the remainder to "A's children then living" is void.

But consider one other "unborn widow" conveyance:

O to A for life, then to A's widow for life, then to A's children.

This conveyance looks just like the one we just worked with except the remainder to A's children is not contingent on surviving A's widow. Therefore, when will that interest vest and close? Immediately on A's death. And since A is a life in being, this remainder is valid.

▶ **5. An identified event that normally would happen well within 21 years, but might not.**

Step 1:

O to A for life, | then to B for 20 years, | then to whoever has received A's land in the distribution of A's estate. |

A has a possessory estate in life estate;

B has a vested remainder for a term of years;

The recipient of A's land has a contingent remainder in fee simple absolute;

O has a reversion in fee simple absolute.

Steps 2 & 3: The contingent remainder is vulnerable.

Step 4: The contingent remainder will vest as soon as A's estate has been distributed.

Step 5: Lives in being: O, A, and B.

---

[47] See page 138.

Step 6: Normally, the assets of an estate are distributed sooner than 21 years after the decedent's death. However, we have no guarantee that A's assets will be distributed ever, let alone by any particular time. It is possible that all lives in being could die, 21 years could go by, and we'd still be waiting to see if A's assets would ever be distributed. The remainder is void.

▶ **6. The holder won't be identified until the death of someone merely described rather than named.**

Step 1:

> ***O to A for life, then to A's first child for life, | then to whoever is the President of the United States. |***
>
> [At present, A has no children.]

A has a possessory estate in life estate;

A's first child has a contingent remainder in life estate;

The President has a contingent remainder in fee simple absolute;

O has a reversion in fee simple absolute.

Steps 2 & 3: The vulnerable interests are the remainder to A's first child and the remainder to the President.

Step 4: The remainder to A's first child will either vest or fail at least by the time A dies. The remainder to the President will vest or fail when A and A's first child (if any) die.

Step 5: Lives in being: O and A.

Step 6: The remainder to A's first child does not violate the Rule because the longest we will have to wait to learn its fate is until A dies, and A is a life in being.

The remainder to the President is different, however. Consider this scenario: After the conveyance, A could have a child (B), who will not be a life in being. Then all lives in being could die. This is when the 21-year clock begins to tick. But we won't know who will be the President when B dies until B actually dies. Could B, who now has a possessory estate in life estate, live longer than 21 years? Yes. In that case, it could be longer than 21 years before we know who (if anyone) will be the President of the United States when B dies. The second contingent remainder violates the Rule.

▶ Analyzing Various Kinds of Future Interests

For more practice, we'll work through some examples of the kinds of grantee future interests we've studied.

▶ Example 1—Vested Remainder (Closed).

O to A for life, then to B.

First, identify the state of the title:

A has a possessory estate in life estate;

B has a vested remainder in fee simple absolute.

In steps 2 and 3, you find a future interest in a grantee (B), but it's already vested and closed. B is ascertained, and no event could prevent B (or B's successors) from taking possession after A dies. This is not a class gift, so the interest is closed. We're not waiting to see if anyone else will qualify to take part of the interest. Therefore, you know that B's interest does not violate the Rule.

▶ Example 2A—Vested Remainder (Subject to Open)—Valid.

*O to A for life, then to all those in O's Property
class who pass the Bar.*

[O took Property 4 years ago. All but five of the students in
the class have passed the Bar.]

First, identify the state of the title:

A has a possessory estate in life estate;

The members of O's Property class who have passed the Bar have a vested remainder in fee simple subject to open.

In steps 2 and 3, you find a future interest in a class of grantees. It is already vested, but it is subject to open. What is the longest time we might have to wait to see who will ultimately pass the Bar? Either when the last Property class member passes the Bar or when the last

Property class member who has not yet passed the Bar dies. At that point, we will know precisely who will qualify for the remainder. Now compare that timing to the permitted time period, remembering who the lives in being are (O, A, and all members of O's Property class). We'll know the complete list of those entitled to the remainder by the time the last Property class member dies, if not before. Therefore, we'll know well before the permitted time expires. The remainder does not violate the Rule.

▶ **Example 2B—Vested Remainder (Subject to Open)—Invalid.**

O to A for life, then to O's children who pass the Bar.

[At present, O has two children (B and C). B has passed the
Bar, and C (who is 15 years old) has not.]

First, identify the state of the title:

A has a possessory estate in life estate;

B has a vested remainder in fee simple (subject to open).

In steps 2 and 3, you find a future interest in a class of grantees. It is already vested, but it is subject to open. What is the longest time we might have to wait to see which of A's children will ultimately pass the Bar? A's death will tell us decisively who A's children are. But unless they have all passed the Bar at that point, we'll have to wait to see how many do. Might we have to wait too long? If A didn't have any more children after the conveyance, then the only possible class members are B and C. Since both are lives in being, the remainder would seem to be OK.

But what if A had another child (D) after the conveyance? D would not be a life in being. Yet, if D passed the Bar, D would become a member of the class. After D was born, O, A, B, and C could die. Might D ultimately pass the Bar? Yes. Might it take D longer than 21 years to do it? Yes. Therefore, the remainder might remain subject to open longer than the permitted time period. The remainder violates the Rule.

▶ **Example 3A—Contingent Remainder—Valid.**

O to A for life, then to B if B reaches 50.

[B is 10.]

First, identify the state of the title:

A has a possessory estate in life estate;

B has a contingent remainder in fee simple absolute.

O has a reversion in fee simple absolute.

For steps 2 and 3, you identify B's interest and observe that it is contingent, so you'll need to proceed to step 4.

When is the last possible moment B's interest will either vest or fail? Answer: It will vest or fail either when B reaches 50 or when B dies without having reached 50. Compare that timing to the time period the Rule permits: 21 years after the death of the last person living right now. You see that the interest will vest well within that time period. B is the validating life. B's contingent remainder will vest when B turns 50, or it will fail when B dies before reaching 50. Since B is a life in being, B's interest will either vest or fail at least 21 years before the time period expires. Therefore, you know that B's interest is valid.

▶ **Example 3B—Contingent Remainders—Invalid.**

> ### *O to A for life, then to A's first child to reach 50.*
>
> [A has no children.]

First, identify the state of the title:

A has a possessory estate in life estate;

A's first child to reach 50 has a contingent remainder in fee simple absolute.

O has a reversion in fee simple absolute.

From steps 2 and 3, you see that the interest in A's first child to reach 50 is vulnerable to the Rule because its taker is unascertained. You need to proceed to step 4.

When is the last possible moment the taker could be ascertained. Answer: 50 years after A's death. A could have a child and then immediately die. Everyone else in the world could die except that child. The perpetuities clock begins to tick. When the clock stops, 21 years later, A's child will be only 21 years old. At that point, we still won't know whether A's child will reach 50. There is no validating life. Therefore, the interest violates the Rule.

Now what? Return to the conveyance, and strike out the offending interest ("then to A's first child to reach 50"). What remains is "O to A for life." So what is the state of the title after such a conveyance? *A has a possessory estate in life estate, and O has a reversion in fee simple absolute.*

▶ **Example 4A—Executory Interest Following a Determinable Estate— Valid.**

> ### *O to A so long as A does not divorce, but if A divorces, then to B.*

First, identify the state of the title:

A has a possessory estate in fee simple determinable;

B has an executory interest in fee simple absolute.

A's interest is already vested in possession, even though it might end early. B's interest is the one we're concerned about. Is B's interest vested? Is it certain to become possessory someday, or must some event happen first? Before B's interest could become possessory, A must divorce. B's interest is therefore vulnerable to the Rule.

So ask yourself whether there is any possible way that B's interest might still be a contingent interest longer than 21 years after everyone alive today dies. Well, just who is it that can cause B's interest to vest? Whose matrimonial state constitutes the condition? Only A can cause B's interest to vest. And when is the last moment that A might breach this condition? The last moment of A's life. Since A is a life in being, B's interest will either vest before A dies or fail the moment A dies. A is the validating life. B's interest is valid.

▶ **Example 4B—Executory Interest Following a Determinable Estate—Invalid.**

> *O to A while neither A nor any lineal descendant of A has divorced, | but if any such person divorces, then to B. |*

First, identify the state of the title:

A has a possessory estate in fee simple determinable;

B has an executory interest in fee simple absolute.

A's interest is already vested in possession, even though it might end early. B's interest is the one we're concerned about. Is B's interest vested? Is it certain to become possessory someday, or must some event happen first? Before B's interest could become possessory, A or a lineal descendant of A must divorce. B's interest is therefore vulnerable to the Rule.

So ask yourself whether it is possible that B's interest might still be a contingent interest longer than 21 years after everyone alive today dies. Who is it that can cause B's interest to vest or fail? Whose matrimonial state constitutes the condition? Unlike the conveyance in the previous example, either A or any lineal descendant of A any time in the future can cause B's interest to vest. All of the people alive today could die, and more than 21 years could go by, and then some future descendant could divorce. Therefore, we can't be sure that B's interest will either vest or fail within the time period permitted by the Rule. B's interest is void.

So strike out B's interest. The state of the title is this:

A has a possessory estate in fee simple determinable;

O has a possibility of reverter in fee simple absolute.

► **Example 5A—Executory Interest Following an Estate Subject to an Executory Limitation—Valid.**

O to A, but if A divorces, then to B.

First, identify the state of the title:

A has a possessory estate in fee simple subject to an executory limitation;

B has an executory interest in fee simple absolute.

A's interest is already vested in possession, even though it might later be interrupted. What about B's interest? Is it vested? Is it certain to become possessory someday, or must some event happen first? Before B's interest could become possessory, A must divorce. B's interest is therefore vulnerable to the Rule.

So is there any possible way that B's interest might still be a contingent interest longer than 21 years after everyone alive today dies? Who can cause B's interest to vest or fail? Only A. And when is the last moment that A might breach this condition? The last moment of A's life. Since A is a life in being, B's interest will either vest before A dies or fail the moment A dies. Therefore, B's interest is valid.

► **Example 5B—Executory Interest Following an Estate Subject to an Executory Limitation—Invalid.**

O to A, but if A or any of A's lineal descendants divorces, then to B.

First, identify the state of the title:

A has a possessory estate in fee simple subject to an executory limitation;

B has an executory interest in fee simple absolute.

Again, A's interest is already vested in possession, even though it might later be divested. B's interest is the one we're concerned about. Is B's interest certain to become possessory someday, or must some event happen first? Before B's interest could become possessory, A or someone in A's line must divorce. B's interest is therefore vulnerable to the Rule.

So ask yourself whether it is possible that B's interest might still be a contingent interest longer than 21 years after everyone alive today dies. Who can cause B's interest to vest or fail? Whose marital state constitutes the condition? As we saw in example 4B, any person in A's line at any time in the future can cause B's interest to vest. All of the people alive today could die, and more than 21 years could go by, and then some future holder of A's interest could divorce and cause B's contingent interest to vest. Therefore, we can't be sure that B's interest will either vest or fail within the time period permitted by the Rule. B's interest is void.

Now what? Return to the conveyance and strike out B's interest ("but if . . . , then to B"). What remains is "O to A." So what is the state of the title after such a conveyance? *A has a possessory estate in fee simple absolute.*

Notice the different results in examples 4A through 5B, and be sure you understand the reasons for the differences.

Study Questions and Practice Exercises

Practice working with the material in this chapter, and learn it well before you go on to the next chapter. Answer the following questions. Make them into flash cards (*including the number of the exercise so you can identify the question later*), add them to your other cards, shuffle, and practice them all again. If you would like even more practice, include all of the examples from Chapters 13 and 14.

14-1 Name the six RAP danger signs.

For each of the following conveyances, (1) give the state of the title as the conveyance is written; (2) identify all interests vulnerable to the Rule Against Perpetuities; (3) for each, state whether the interest is valid; and (4) give the state of the title if different after applying the Rule.

14-2 O to A for life, then to A's first child to reach age 30. [A has two children: B (25) and C (28).]

14-3 O to A for life, then to A's first child to reach age 21. [A has two children: B (19) and C (18).]

14-4 O to A for life, then to B and her heirs if B reaches 25. (B is now 5.)

14-5 O to A for life, then to A's first child for life, then to B's first child if he or she survives A's first child. (At present, neither A nor B has children.)

14-6 O to A for life, then to A's first child if he survives A by 20 years. (A has no children yet.)

14-7 O to A for life, then to A's first grandchild and his or her heirs. (A has six children and no grandchildren.)

14-8 O devises to A for life, then to O's first grandchild and his or her heirs. (O has six children and no grandchildren.)

14-9 O to A for life, then to B's first child to graduate from law school and his or her heirs. (B has two children; and one of them is a first-year law student.)

14-10 O to A for life, then to the residuary beneficiary under A's will for life, then to that person's children who survive him or her.

14-11 O to A for life, then to the residuary beneficiary under A's will for life, then to that person's children.

14-12 O to A and her heirs as long as the land is used for educational purposes; and if it is not used for educational purposes, then to B and her heirs.

14-13 O devises "to the next President of the United States upon his or her swearing in."

14-14 O to A for life, then to B and her heirs, but if B ever sells liquor on the land, to C and her heirs.

14-15 O to A for life, then to A's children and their heirs.
(a) Assume that A has no children.
(b) Assume that A has one child, X.

14-16 O to A for life, then to A's children who reach age 30. [A has two children: B (30) and C (28).]

14-17 *Here is a modified and condensed version of a mystery titled "Death Makes a Difference," written by Professor Brainerd Currie and published in The Student Lawyer Journal, Feb.–Apr. 1960, 1–17. In this modified version, a murder was committed by the person who had the greatest financial interest in the outcome. Solve the murder.*

"Hello, yes, quick, send an ambulance to 416 Craddock Way. Please hurry!" Jim Brattle hung up the phone and turned again to face the situation he had found when he opened the door. He had come to see his client, Matilda Audley, with the sad news of her brother's death. But when he arrived, he found a horrible sight. Miss Matilda was lying on the floor in front of the hearth with the mantel clock in pieces beside her. She had an open wound on the side of her head. She appeared to be dead.

The ambulance arrived in minutes, but to no avail. Miss Matilda was definitely dead. Her lawyer of many years sank weakly into a chair to contemplate the events. The more he thought about it, the more amazed he was that these two deaths would come so close together. Miss Matilda's brother, Grant Twisden, had suffered a heart attack the week before, and he had been barely clinging to life since then. He had died at 6:15 this evening, and his doctor had called Jim right away.

"Jim, I have some bad news. Grant Twisden has just died. I know you're close to his sister. I understand that Miss Matilda's daughter, Jee, is out of town, and the only other child, a son, lives out of town. The grandson, Jee's son, was here a few minutes ago, but I can't find him now. I don't know who else to call. Would you go tell Miss Matilda about Grant's death? I don't want to tell her by phone. I know she had a stroke recently, and she shouldn't be alone when she hears the news."

Jim had left for Miss Matilda's house right away. He had knocked and waited, but no one came to the door. He stepped to the window, peered in, and saw her there, lying in front of the hearth. He broke in, tried unsuccessfully to find a pulse, and quickly placed the call to 911. The ambulance crew said it looked like she had a stroke, fell and hit her head, knocking the clock to the floor as she fell. They recorded the estimated time of her death as 5:30, according to the time on the broken face of the mantel clock.

Sheriff Jack Thellusson arrived shortly after the ambulance crew, and Jim told him what he knew. The Sheriff thought it sounded strange, too. He and Jim had known each other for 30 years, starting back in the days when the Sheriff had been a rookie cop and Jim had been an up-and-coming young public defender. The Sheriff had developed a grudging respect for Jim in those days, which had ripened into a genuine friendship after Jim had joined a firm and started an estates practice.

Jim had barely had a chance to fill the Sheriff in when Miss Matilda's next door neighbor, Mr. Leake, arrived, carrying a paper bag. Jim looked up and saw the shocked expression on his face.

"What's happened?" he demanded. Jim told him it looked like Miss Matilda had a stroke. "Miss Matilda dead! It doesn't seem possible. I was talking to her less than an hour ago." Jim and the Sheriff exchanged glances.

"You say you were talking to her within the last hour?"

"Right. She called me just before I left work. I own the Village Butcher Shop, and she wanted me to bring her a couple of lamb chops for dinner. When she stopped driving, she got in the habit of asking me to bring her stuff when I came home from work, and I don't mind—uh, I didn't mind, that is."

"What time would you say she called?"

"Well, let's see. It must have been right after 6:00, because I had just locked the door when the phone rang."

The Sheriff took Jim into the hallway. "What do you make of this, Jim? It looks like somebody wanted us to think Matilda died earlier than she did. Do you think this has something to do with her brother's death? Would it be important somehow whether she predeceased him?"

"I don't know, Jack. But I think it bears looking into. I drafted Miss Matilda's will, and I can tell you she didn't have anything to leave anybody. Her will gives this old house to her two kids, Jee and Barton, but that's about all there was. And this house is more of a liability than an asset. I'll tell you what. Why don't you get me a copy of Grant Twisden's will. I'll bet his estate is worth about three million. Let's see what his will says."

"Good idea. I'll see if I can get it tomorrow morning, and I'll bring it to your office right away."

The next morning, the Sheriff dropped by Jim's office with a copy of Grant Twisden's will. Jim skimmed through the usual boiler-plate clauses until he came to the dispositional clause. He read it carefully. It said, "I leave three million dollars in trust, and I direct the trustees to pay the income to my sister Matilda's children for their lives. On their deaths, I direct my trustee to dissolve the trust and pay over the principle to their children. After these bequests have been made, I leave whatever is left of my estate to the Bibb County Food Bank."

Jim was quiet for a few minutes. Then he said, "Jack, I have a theory . . . ."

Relief from the Rule Against Perpetuities

This last chapter in our study of the Rule Against Perpetuities describes three ways a conveyance can be relieved from the common law Rule Against Perpetuities: (1) by the application of the doctrine of the destructibility of contingent remainders; (2) by the application of the charitable exemption; and (3) by modern statutory modifications to the Rule. If your class did not study the doctrine of the destructibility of contingent remainders, simply omit the following discussion of that doctrine and the practice exercises that apply it.

▶ The Effect of the Destructibility of Contingent Remainders Doctrine

As you recall from Chapter 11, the doctrine of destructibility of contingent remainders destroys any remainders that are still contingent when the prior estate ends. For example, consider the following conveyance:

> ***O to A for life, then to A's first child to graduate from law school.***
>
> [A has no child who has graduated from law school.]

When A dies, if no child of A has graduated from law school, the contingent remainder is destroyed.

In a jurisdiction that applies the doctrine of destructibility of contingent remainders, the doctrine can sometimes save a conveyance from the effects of the Rule Against Perpetuitites. For instance, consider the conveyance above. If we apply the Rule Against Perpetuities to that conveyance, the contingent remainder would seem to be void. A might have an afterborn child (X) who might graduate from law school longer than 21 years after all lives in being have died.

But in a jurisdiction that applies destructibility, the contingent remainder would be valid. In such a jurisdiction, the contingent remainder would *either* vest during A's lifetime *or* be destroyed when A died. It could not still be contingent after A's life estate ended.

Here is another example:

O to A for life, then to B's first child to reach 30.

[B has no children.]

A has a possessory estate in life estate, B's first child to reach 30 has a contingent remainder, and O has a reversion. If we do not apply the destructibility doctrine, the contingent remainder violates the Rule Against Perpetuities. B could have a child (C) immediately after the conveyance was made. Then A, B, and everyone else except C could die. The clock starts ticking. When it strikes, 21 years later, C would be only 21 years old, and the remainder would still be contingent, waiting for C to reach 30. Therefore, the remainder is invalid.

However, in a jurisdiction that destroys remainders that are still contingent at the termination of the prior estate, we would know the fate of the remainder immediately on A's death. If no child of B's had reached 30 by the time A died, the remainder would be destroyed. Therefore, it wouldn't be possible for the remainder to still be contingent 21 years after the death of A (or any other life in being). The remainder would not violate the Rule. The remainder would be valid at the time of the conveyance. It might be destroyed later, but only if it didn't vest by the time A died.

► The Charitable Exemption

If *both* the possessory estate and the vulnerable future interest are given to charitable organizations, the Rule Against Perpetuities does not apply. The future interest given to the second charity is valid. For example, consider the following conveyance:

O to A, but if the land is ever leased to another grantee, then to Planned Parenthood.

Here the executory interest given to Planned Parenthood would violate the Rule Against Perpetuities. Hundreds of years from now, some future successor to A could lease the land and therefore trigger the executory interest. Since the executory interest could still be burdening the land for well beyond the permitted period, the interest would be void under the Rule.

However, if both the possessory estate and the future interest are given to a charitable organization, the Rule does not apply. For instance:

O to the Easter Seals, but if the land is ever leased to another grantee, then to Planned Parenthood.

Here both the possessory estate and the future interest are given to charities. The exemption applies, and the executory interest is valid.

▶ Statutory Modifications of the Rule Against Perpetuities

Many jurisdictions have adopted one of two modern variations on the Rule Against Perpetuities. In one such variation, we can "wait and see" whether the interest will vest and close during the common law's permitted time period (21 years after the death of a life in being). Only if the future interest does not vest and close (or fail) within the common law's permitted time period is the interest destroyed. For example, consider the following conveyance:

O to A for life, then to A's first child to reach 30.

[A has one child, B, who is 10.]

Under the common law version of the Rule, the contingent remainder would be void. A might have an afterborn child, and A and B might die soon thereafter. The afterborn child might reach 30, and it would take longer than 21 years to know.

However, in a "wait for the common law time period" jurisdiction, we can allow the contingent remainder to wait until 21 years after the death of all lives in being (those who can affect vesting). A remainder that has not either vested and closed or failed by that time is destroyed.[48]

A variation on the "wait and see" doctrine allows us to wait for a set period of time after the conveyance, generally 90 years. From the drafter's perspective, this approach has the great virtue of eliminating the need to identify lives in being and calculate a different permitted time period for each conveyance. In jurisdictions that take this approach, the contingent remainder above would be valid for 90 years. If it had neither vested and closed nor failed by then, it would be destroyed.[49]

The primary difference between these modern variations and the original Rule is, of course, that the original Rule does not allow us to wait

---

[48] In some jurisdictions, a court will reform the interest to approximate as closely as possible the grantor's intention.

[49] Or reformed. See note 47.

to see whether the interest will vest within the permitted time period. According to the original form of the Rule, if there is any possible scenario in which the interest might still be contingent at the end of the permitted time period, the interest is struck at the moment of the conveyance.

▶ Study Questions and Practice Exercises

Practice working with the material in this chapter before you go on to the next chapter. Answer the following questions, using the chart to help you. Make them into flash cards (*including the number of the exercise so you can identify the question later*), add them to your other cards, shuffle, and practice them all again.

For each interest that is vulnerable to the Rule Against Perpetuities, state whether the interest is valid or void. If your class studied the doctrine of destructibility of contingent remainders, assume that the doctrine applies. If your class did not study the doctrine, ignore it.

15-1 O to A for 10 years, then to the first of A's children to join a law enforcement agency. (At present, A has no children.)

15-2 O to A, but if the land is ever not farmed, then to Habitat for Humanity.

15-3 O to Food for the World, but if the land is ever not farmed, then to Habitat for Humanity.

15-4 O to A for life, then to B's first grandchild. (At present, B has two children and no grandchildren.)

Putting It All Together

16

In the last five chapters, we have covered a number of doctrines. This chapter will draw them all together and give you an approach for accounting for all of these doctrines when you analyze a conveyance.

If your Property class did not cover any of these doctrines, simply ignore the references to that doctrine. The answers to the Study Questions and Practice Exercises in Appendix C will identify which doctrines you'll need to know to answer which questions, so you can tell which questions to omit.

First, a recap:

Recap of Doctrines Affecting Conveyances

The Rule in Shelley's Case

$$O \text{ to } A \text{ for life, then to } \text{~~A's heirs~~ } \underline{A}.$$

The Doctrine of Worthier Title

$$O \text{ to } A \text{ for life, then to } \text{~~O's heirs~~ } \underline{O}.$$

Merger
When a life estate and the next vested estate come into the hands of the same person, they are combined. If they are separated by a contingent remainder, the remainder is destroyed.

Destruction of Contingent Remainders
A remainder that is still contingent at the end of the prior estate will be destroyed.

The Rule Against Perpetuities
No interest is good unless it must either fail or vest and close within 21 years of the death of a life in being.

You may be wondering how to apply all of these doctrines to the same conveyance. Actually, the answer is not difficult. Here is a procedure for analyzing a conveyance with all of these doctrines in mind:

Applying Multiple Doctrines

At the Time of the Conveyance

1. Apply the Rule in Shelley's Case (and merger, if applicable) to any offending grantee interest.

2. Apply the doctrine of worthier title (and merger, if applicable) to any offending interest given to the grantor's heirs.

3. Apply the Rule Against Perpetuities to any vulnerable contingent or open grantee interest (keeping in mind that a contingent remainder might be saved if the jurisdiction applies the doctrine of destruction of contingent remainders).

After Subsequent Factual Developments

4. Apply merger to any vested interests that come into the hands of the same person and are not separated by another vested estate.

5. Apply the doctrine of destruction of contingent remainders to any remainder still contingent at the close of the prior estate.

▶ **Example 1.**

> *O to A for life, then to A's heirs, but if the land is ever used other than for a single-family residence, then to B.*

1. Apply the Rule in Shelley's Case (and merger):

> *O to A, but if the land is ever used other than for a single-family residence, then to B.*

2. The doctrine of worthier title doesn't apply.

3. The Rule Against Perpetuities invalidates B's executory interest. Now A has a possessory estate in fee simple absolute.

▶ **Example 2.**

> *O to A for life, then to A's first grandchild.*
>
> [A has no children or grandchildren.]

Subsequently, O dies, devising all his property to A.

1. Shelley's Case doesn't apply.

2. Worthier title doesn't apply.

3. The contingent remainder to A's first grandchild is invalidated by the Rule Against Perpetuities (unless the jurisdiction applies the doctrine of destruction of contingent remainders). Assuming a jurisdiction without the doctrine:

   A has a life estate;

   O has a reversion in fee simple absolute.

4. When O dies, apply merger:

   A has a fee simple absolute.

▶ **Example 3.**

O to A for life, then to O's heirs.

1. Shelley's Case doesn't apply.

2. Apply the doctrine of worthier title: *O to A for life, then to O.*

3. The Rule Against Perpetuities doesn't apply, because O's remainder is vested and closed.

▶ **Example 4.**

O to A for life, then to A's heirs if B dies childless.
[B has no children.]

Subsequently, A dies. B still has no children.

1. Apply the Rule in Shelley's Case:

   ### *O to A for life, then to A if B dies childless.*

   Merger doesn't combine a life estate with a contingent interest.

2. Worthier title doesn't apply.

3. A has a contingent remainder, but it will fail or vest at least by B's death. The Rule Against Perpetuities doesn't invalidate A's interest.

4. No merger: No post-conveyance facts have brought a life estate and a vested interest into the hands of the same person.

5. On A's death, the doctrine of destruction of contingent remainders would destroy the contingent remainder to A (now held by A's successors) rather than waiting until B either had a child or died childless. Therefore, *O has a possessory estate in fee simple absolute.*

▶ Study Questions and Practice Exercises

Practice working with the material in this chapter, and learn it well. Answer the following questions, using the chart to help you. Make them into flash cards (*including the number of the exercise so you can identify the question later*), add them to your other cards, shuffle, and practice them all again.

For all of the following conveyances, apply all of the doctrines and rules we have studied. Consult Appendix C if your Property class did not cover all of these doctrines. If the question contains more than one transfer or factual development, your answer should classify the interests as they stand at the conclusion of all of the transfers and factual developments.

16-1 O to A for life, then to B and his heirs, then to C and his heirs.

16-2 O to A for life, then to B's heirs, then to C's heirs.

16-3 O to A and her heirs as long as the land is used for educational purposes.

16-4 O to A and her heirs as long as the land is used for educational purposes, but if the land is not used for educational purposes, then to B and his heirs.

16-5 O to A and her heirs, but if she stops using the land for educational purposes, then to O.

16-6 O to A if she graduates from law school. (A has not yet graduated from law school.)

16-7 O to A for life, then to B if B survives A, but if B does not survive A, to C's children. (C has one child, X.)

16-8 O to A for life, then to A's heirs.

16-9 *First conveyance:*   O to A for life, then to B and her heirs.
       Second conveyance: A to C.

16-10 *First conveyance:*   O to A for life, then to B if B survives A.
       Second conveyance: O conveys to A.

16-11 O to A for life, then to B if B marries. (B is unmarried.) Subsequently, A dies and B is still unmarried.

16-12 O to A for life, then to B if B adopts A's surviving children.

16-13 O to A for life, then to O's heirs.

16-14 O to A for life, then to A's widow for life, then to A's children who survive A's widow. [A is now married and has a child (B).]

16-15 *First conveyance:*   O to A for life.
        Second conveyance: O to B and C.

16-16 O to A for life, then to A's children. (A has one child, B.)

16-17 *First conveyance:*   O to A for life, then to B, but if B sells liquor on the premises, to O.
        Second conveyance: A inherits from O.

16-18 *First conveyance:*   O to A for life, then to B.
        Second conveyance: B conveys to O's heirs.

16-19 O to A for life, then to B's heirs, and if B has no heirs, then to C. (Then A dies and B is still alive.)

16-20 O to A for life, then to B's heirs, and if B has no heirs, then to C. (Then B dies with heirs. Then A dies.)

16-21 O to A for life, then to B if B graduates from law school, but if B does not graduate from law school, then to C. (Then A dies. B is two weeks away from graduating from law school.)

16-22 O to A for life, then to B's first child to become a doctor. (B has two children, ages 2 and 5.)

16-23 O devises to A for life, then to A's first grandchild. (A has three children and two grandchildren.)

16-24 O to A for life, then to A's heirs.

16-25 O to A for life, then to B for life, then to A's heirs.

16-26 O to A for life, then to A's first child to reach 25. (A has no children.)

16-27 State the order in which the Chapter 11-15 rules and doctrines should be applied.

16-28 Which rules and doctrines apply immediately at the creation of a conveyance?

16-29 Which rules and doctrines apply after subsequent factual developments?

An Alternative Outline of Estates and Future Interests

POSSESSORY ESTATE

Nature of Possessory Estate

1. What is the nature of the possessory estate?

    fee simple (has no inherent end)

    > ***O to A and her heirs.***

    fee tail (passes to issue until the line runs out)

    > ***O to A and the heirs of her body.***

    life estate (ends when the measuring life dies)

    > ***O to A for life.***

    term of years (ends after a designated period of time)

    > ***O to A for 10 years.***

Added Limitation

2. If there is *no* added limitation on the duration of the possessory estate, here are your two choices:

Fee simple	add **absolute**
Fee tail, life estate, or **term of years**	add no term

3. If there *is* an added limitation on the duration of the possessory estate, add one of these terms to the name of the estate:

   Add **determinable** if the added limitation
   - is placed within the description of the possessory estate itself; and
   - uses terms like *until, so long as, while,* or *during.*

   Add **subject to a condition subsequent** if
   - the added condition is placed in the description of the *next* interest;
   - it uses terms like *but if, provided that, on condition that,* or *however*; and
   - the next future interest is held by *the grantor.*

   Add **subject to an executory limitation** if
   - the added condition is placed in the description of the *next* interest;
   - it uses terms like *but if, provided that, on condition that* or *however*; and
   - the next future interest is held by *another grantee.*

FUTURE INTEREST

Kind of Future Interest

1. If the possessory estate is a *fee simple absolute,* no future interest will follow it chronologically.

2. If the possessory estate is a *fee tail, life estate,* or *term of years,* here are the kinds of future interests that can follow it:

   Reversion held by *the grantor*
   Remainder held by *another grantee*

   - **Vested**
   - **Vested subject to divestment**
   - **Contingent**

3. If the possessory estate is a *fee simple determinable,* here are the kinds of future interests that follow it:

   Possibility of reverter   held by *the grantor*
   Executory interest   held by *another grantee*

4. If the possessory estate is a *fee simple subject to a condition subsequent,* the future interest that follows it will be a **possibility of reverter**, held by *the grantor.*

5. If the possessory estate is a *fee simple subject to an executory limitation,* the future interest that follows it will be an **execu-**

tory interest, held by *another grantee*. Here are the two kinds of executory interests:

Shifting executory interest   follows an interest held by *a grantee*
Springing executory interest   divests an interest held by *the grantor*

Nature of Future Estate

6. What is the nature of this future interest?

    fee simple (has no inherent end)

    ### O to A and her heirs.

    fee tail (passes to issue until the line runs out)

    ### O to A and the heirs of her body.

    life estate (ends when the measuring life dies)

    ### O to A for life.

    term of years (ends after a designated period of time)

    ### O to A for 10 years.

Added Limitation

7. If there is *no* added limitation on the duration of this future interest, here are your two choices:

    Fee simple   add **absolute**
    Fee tail, life estate, or **term of years**   add no term

8. If there *is* an added limitation on the duration of this future interest, add one of these terms to the name of the estate:

    Add **determinable** if the added limitation
    - is placed within the description of the this future interest itself; and
    - uses terms like *until, so long as, while,* or *during.*

    Add **subject to a condition subsequent** if
    - the added condition is placed in the description of the *next* future interest;
    - it uses terms like *but if, provided that, on condition that,* or *however*; and
    - the next future interest is held by *the grantor.*

Add **subject to an executory limitation** if
- the added condition is placed in the description of the *next* future interest;
- it uses terms like *but if, provided that, on condition that, or however*; and
- the next future interest is held by *another grantee*.

Vocabulary

Be sure to learn the following terms. Page numbers on which the terms are discussed and defined are included with each entry.

absolute   An estate without any limitations at all (with no inherent limitations and no added limitations). Only a fee simple can be "absolute." *(p. 21)*

alienable   A property interest that can be conveyed to another person is alienable. *(p. 120)*

ancestor   A relative from whom one is descended in a direct line (parents, grandparents, great-grandparents, and on back in one's family line). *(p. 4)*

alternative contingent remainder   A pair of remainders with opposite conditions precedent. *(p. 65)*

ascertained   The holder of a future interest is ascertained if that person is alive and identified. (The heirs of a living person are not ascertained. Neither is that person's widow, widower, or devisees.) *(p. 57)*

bequeath   To give an item of personal property or by will. *(p. 4)*

bequest   An item of personal property or interest given by will. *(p. 4)*

collaterals   Relatives other than ancestors and issue. Collaterals include siblings, aunts, uncles, and cousins. *(p. 4)*

condition precedent   A condition (other than the termination of the prior estate) that must be fulfilled before a future interest-holder's right to eventual possession is assured. If a condition must be fulfilled before the remainder-holder can be assured of the right to possession upon the termination of the prior estate and if the condition is placed within the description of the remainder, the remainder is said to be contingent upon the fulfillment of the condition precedent. *(p. 56)*

contingent remainder   A remainder that has one or both of the following characteristics: (1) It is given to an unascertained person; and (2) it contains a condition precedent, that is, a condition (other than the termination of the prior estate) that must be satisfied before the interest can become possessory. *(p. 55)*

convey   To transfer a property interest to another, either by sale or by gift. *(p. 4)*

decedent   A person who has died. *(p. 4)*

defeasible estate   The name for the category of estates that could end early by the happening of a particular event. Two kinds of defeasible estates are *determinable* estates and estates *subject to a condition subsequent*. *(p. 23)*

destructibility of contingent remainders (doctrine of)   A doctrine that provides that a contingent remainder is destroyed if it is still contingent when the prior estate ends. *(p. 121)*

determinable   An estate is determinable if the grantor has described its duration as measured by the occurrence of a particular condition or event. *Example*: "O to A until B reaches 30." If the limiting condition or event (B reaching 30) is not described in the part of the conveyance that creates the interest limited by it, the limited estate is not determinable. An example of a conveyance in which the limitation is not a determinable limitation is "O to A, but if B reaches 30, then to B." *(p. 23)*

It is a common drafting custom to place the determinable limitation before the comma that marks the end of the description of the determinable estate and to place the limitation after that comma if the limitation is not a determinable limitation.

devise   A gift of an interest in real property given by a decedent's will. *(p. 4)*

devisee   The recipient of a gift of an interest in real property given by a decedent's will. *(p. 4)*

disentail   To convert a fee tail estate into a fee simple estate. Also known as "barring an entail." *(p. 116)*

doctrine of worthier title   A doctrine that creates a presumption that a grantor who conveys a future interest to his or her own heirs actually intended to reserve that interest in himself or herself. For example, in the conveyance "O to A for life, then to O's heirs," the doctrine would read the identity of the future interest holder as "O" instead of

"O's heirs." This presumption can be overcome with sufficient evidence of a contrary intent on the part of O. *(p. 130)*

escheat   If a decedent has no heirs or devisees, the interest in land "escheats" (passes) to the state. *(p. 4)*

executory interest   A future interest created in a grantee and following an estate that might end before its natural duration by the occurrence of a particular event or condition. The description of the event or condition can actually define the prior estate's duration, or it can be described as part of the executory interest interrupting the prior estate. *Examples:* "O to A until B reaches 30, then to B," and "O to A, but when B reaches 30, then to B." *(p. 72)*

fee simple   An interest that can, theoretically, continue forever. A fee simple can be contrasted with a fee tail (which ends on the termination of the holder's lineal descendants), a life estate (which ends when the measuring life dies), and a term of years (which ends when the lease term expires). *(p. 9)*

fee tail   An interest that passes automatically to the holder's issue (lineal descendants) upon the holder's death and that ends when the last lineal descendant dies. *(p. 10)*

future interest   A right to future possession. The right can be conditioned on the occurrence of a certain event or condition, or it can be unconditional. *(p. 7)*

grantee   A person who receives, by gift or sale, an interest in property. *(p. 2)*

grantor   The person who transfers, by gift or sale, an interest in property. *(p. 2)*

heirs   The people who receive the property of a person who has died without a will. Heirs are defined by statute. *(p. 4)*

intestate   A person dies intestate if he or she dies without a will. *(p. 4)*

issue   A person's lineal descendants (children, grandchildren, great-grandchildren, etc.). *(p. 4)*

life estate   An interest that will end upon the death of the person whose life is designated as the measuring life. *Examples:* "O to A for life" and "O to A for the life of B." *(p. 12)*

life estate pur autre vie   A life estate measured by the life of another. A life estate pur autre vie can be created at the time of the creation of the life estate ("O to A for the life of B") or by later conveyance of the life estate ("O, who holds a life estate, conveys that life estate to A.") *(p. 15)*

lineal descendants   A person's direct descendants (issue). Examples are children, grandchildren, and great-grandchildren. Relatives who are not lineal descendants are ancestors (parents, grandparents, etc.) and collaterals (siblings, aunts, uncles, cousins, etc.). *(p. 4)*

lives in being   Persons who are alive at the time of the conveyance. *(p. 141)*

merger   A doctrine that combines a lesser vested estate into a larger vested estate when the two estates come into the hands of the same person and are not separated by another vested estate. *(pp. 118, 129, 132)*

possessory estate   The holder of the possessory estate has the current (as opposed to a future) right to possess the land. The opposite of a possessory estate is a future interest. *(p. 7)*

possibility of reverter   A future interest retained by the grantor and following a determinable estate. *Example:* "O to A until B reaches 30, then back to O." *(p. 42)*

pur autre vie   Literally "for the life of another." A life estate pur autre vie is a life estate that lasts for the duration of the life of another. *(p. 15)*

remainder   A future interest given to a grantee and following an estate that will end naturally. Remainders follow fee tail estates, life estates, and terms of years. *Example:* "O to A for life, then to B." Contrast a remainder with a reversion, which is the same future interest except that it is retained by the grantor. *(p. 52)*

reversion   A future interest retained by the grantor and following an estate that will end naturally. Reversions follow fee tail estates, life estates, and terms of years. *Example:* "O to A for life, then back to O." Contrast a reversion with a remainder, which is the same future interest except that it is held by a grantee. *(p. 41)*

right of entry   A future interest retained by the grantor and following an estate subject to a condition subsequent. *Example:* "O to A, but if A uses the land for a tavern, then back to O." *(p. 44)*

Rule Against Perpetuities   The doctrine that strikes down the conveyance of a contingent or open interest if that interest might still be contingent or open longer than 21 years after the death of the last life in being at the creation of the interest. *Example:* "O to A, but if the land is ever used for a tavern, then to B." B's interest is invalid because it might still be a contingent interest for generations into the future. *(pp. 135, 140)*

Rule in Shelley's Case   A doctrine that prohibited the conveyance of a future interest to the heirs of the grantee receiving the possessory estate. If the grantor attempted to convey a future interest to that grantee's heirs, the interest was read as in the grantee rather than in the grantee's heirs. *Example:* "O to A for life, then to A's heirs" would be read instead as "O to A for life, then to A." (The doctrine of merger would then cause the life estate to merge into the future interest, and A would have a possessory estate in fee simple absolute.) *(p. 127)*

seisin   The right to possession of land accompanied by particular responsibilities, such as the payment of taxes. *(p. 13)*

Shelley's Case   See "Rule in Shelley's Case." *(p. 127)*

shifting executory interest   An executory interest that follows an interest held by another grantee. *(p. 95)*

springing executory interest   An executory interest that follows an interest held by the grantor. *(p. 95)*

subject to a condition subsequent   An estate whose natural duration may be cut short by the happening of a particular event or condition allowing the grantor to retake the property. The event or condition is described as a part of the grantor's future interest rather than as part of the estate it may cut short. *Example:* "O to A, but if A uses the property for a tavern, then back to O." *(p. 23)*

subject to divestment   See "vested remainder subject to divestment." *(p. 89)*

subject to an executory limitation   An estate is subject to an executory limitation if it is followed by an interest in a grantee and if it can be interrupted by the occurrence of a particular event or condition not described directly as the measurement of the estate's duration. Rather, the limiting event or condition is described as part of the following future interest interrupting the prior estate. *Example:* "O to A, but when B reaches 30, then to B." *(p. 75)*

subject to open   An estate is subject to open if it is given to a class of persons and if one or more of those persons is already ascertained as part of the class but others could be added. *Example:* "O to A (who is alive and has one child, B), then to A's children." The future interest held by B (in his capacity as A's child) is subject to open because A could have more children. *(p. 93)*

subject to partial divestment   A synonym for "subject to open." *(p. 93)*

term of years   A lease for a designated period of time. *(p. 13)*

testate   A person dies testate if he or she dies with a will. *(p. 4)*

validating life   A person who proves that an interest will either vest and close or fail within the time period permitted by the Rule Against Perpetuities. *(p. 143)*

vested remainder   A remainder that has an ascertained taker and no condition precedent. *(p. 55)*

vested remainder subject to divestment   A remainder that is vested (has an ascertained taker and is not subject to a condition precedent) but could later be divested before it ever becomes possessory. If the divesting condition could happen before the vested remainder becomes possessory, the remainder is subject to divestment. Here is an example of a vested remainder subject to divestment: "O to A for life, then to B, but if B does not survive A, then to C." B's remainder is vested because there is no condition precedent *contained within the language creating B's interest.* However, if B dies before A, B's remainder will be divested. The language creating this condition is located in C's interest rather than in B's interest. If the condition had been contained within the language creating B's interest ("then to B if B survives A"), B's interest would be subject to a condition precedent and would therefore be a contingent remainder rather than a vested remainder subject to divestment. *(p. 89)*

words of limitation   The part of a conveyance that identifies the nature of the estate conveyed. In the conveyance "O to A and her heirs," the words of limitation are "and her heirs," indicating that A is receiving a fee simple. *(p. 9)*

words of purchase   The part of a conveyance that identifies the grantee. In the conveyance "O to A and her heirs," the words of purchase are "to A." *(p. 9)*

worthier title (doctrine of)   See "doctrine of worthier title." *(p. 130)*

Answers to Study Questions and Practice Exercises

CHAPTER 1

1-1 Collaterals

1-2 A beneficiary of real property under a will.

1-3 "Heirs" are those who take in the absence of a will. "Devisees" are those who take under a will.

1-4 Devise

1-5 Intestate

1-6 To "convey" includes both transfer by sale and transfer by gift.

1-7 Decedent

1-8 Siblings, aunts, uncles, cousins, nieces, nephews

1-9 A "devisee" is one who receives real property under a will. Maude is the "heir" of Harold's estate.

1-10 Issue

1-11 Ancestors

1-12 Bequest

1-13 Testate

1-14 Children, grandchildren, great-grandchildren

1-15 Escheat

1-16 A living person has no heirs.

1-17 None. A will creates no interests in property until the testator dies.

CHAPTER 2

2-1 Words of purchase

2-2 Words of limitation

2-3 O to A and her heirs, (fee simple)

2-4 O to A (for 2 years.) (term of years)

2-5 O to A (and the heirs of his body.) (fee tail)

2-6 O to A (for life.) (life estate)

2-7 O to A (for the life of B.) (life estate pur autre vie)

2-8 O to A. (Assume modern law.) (fee simple)

2-9 A has a fee simple. B has nothing.

2-10 B has a life estate pur autre vie. A is the measuring life. B's life estate will last until A dies.

2-11 A (the owner of a fee tail in its original form) can convey only the right to possess the land during A's life. Therefore, B's estate will last only until A dies.

2-12 B's estate will last for the remainder of the 10 years.

2-13 B's estate ends when A dies.

2-14 B's estate is unaffected by A's death. B has one more year of possession left.

2-15 B's estate ended in 1995.

2-16 B has no estate. Upon the death of the holder, a fee tail passes automatically to the holder's issue without regard to the terms of the holder's will. C has the right to possession.

2-17 B has no estate. Upon the death of A, the life estate ended.

2-18 Only A has an interest.

2-19 Only A has an interest.

2-20 Only A has an interest.

2-21 Only A has an interest.

2-22 Only C has an interest.

2-23 A has a term of years. O has the right to possession after A's term of years ends.

2-24 A has a fee tail. O has the right to possession after A's issue die out.

2-25 A has a life estate. O has the right to possession after A dies.

2-26 A has a fee simple. No one else has a right to possession either now or in the future.

2-27 A has a life estate pur autre vie. O has the right to possession after B (the measuring life) dies.

2-28 A has a fee simple. No one else has a right to possession either now or in the future.

2-29 "Yes, you should be concerned. If your lessor has only a life estate in the property, your lease will end when your lessor dies. Even if your lessor is young and healthy, accidents happen. You don't want to invest a lot of money in improvements to the property without knowing whether you'll be able to recoup the investment. The first thing to do is to confirm that your lessor has only a life estate. If so, you should find out who owns the other interests in the property. If you can negotiate a leasehold interest from all other owners, you can proceed safely. If not, you should reconsider."

2-30 "You can grant your husband a life estate in the property now. Then you can devise all your remaining interest in the property to your son. If you don't want to dispose of your possessory estate before you die, you can devise a life estate to your husband and devise all remaining interest to your son." (*There are several way to accomplish the client's goal. The answer above sets out a way that uses the material we have studied in this chapter.*)

2-31 "No, Bob isn't right, and you can rent the house. When your husband devised all of his other property to Bob, Bob received the right to the house after you die. However, as long as you live, you have the possessory estate, and that right includes the right to lease it to someone else. If you were to die during the lease period, your tenant's rights under the lease would end though, so you'll want to be candid with a prospective tenant about that possibility. As a practical matter, that possibility might affect your market and perhaps the amount of rent you can expect, but you may well find a tenant who isn't concerned about the possibility of having to move at some point."

CHAPTER 3

3-1 Only a fee simple can be absolute.

3-2 Fee tail, life estate, and term of years

3-3 Fee tail, life estate, and term of years

3-4 A determinable estate

3-5 An estate subject to a condition subsequent

3-6 Until, while, during, as long as

3-7 But if, provided that, on condition that, however

3-8 An estate subject to a condition subsequent

3-9 Determinable estate

3-10 An estate subject to a condition subsequent

3-11 O to A so long as A does not divorce B, | then back to O.
A: possessory estate in fee simple determinable

3-12 O to A and her heirs so long as A does not divorce B, | but if A divorces B, then back to O.
A: possessory estate in fee simple determinable

3-13 O to A and his heirs, | but if A divorces B, then to O.
A: possessory estate in fee simple subject to a condition subsequent

3-14 O to A, | on the condition that A does not divorce B.
A: possessory estate in fee simple subject to a condition subsequent

3-15 O to A and his heirs, | provided that A does not divorce B, then to O.
A: possessory estate in fee simple subject to a condition subsequent

3-16 O to A until A divorces B, | then back to O.
A: possessory estate in fee simple determinable

3-17 O to A; | however, if A divorces B, then to O.
A: possessory estate in fee simple subject to a condition subsequent

3-18 O to A and her heirs while A refrains from divorcing B. |
A: possessory estate in fee simple determinable

3-19 O to A and her heirs during the time that A refrains from divorcing B, | then back to O.
A: has a possessory estate in fee simple determinable

3-20 O to A. | (Assume modern law.)
A: possessory estate in fee simple absolute

3-21 O to A, | provided that A never drills for oil on the property.
A: possessory estate in fee simple subject to a condition subsequent

3-22 O to A and his heirs for so long as A cares for B on the premises. |
A: possessory estate in fee simple determinable

3-23 O to A for life or until B graduates from medical school. |
A: possessory estate in life estate determinable

3-24 O to A and the heirs of his body. |
A: possessory estate in fee tail

3-25 O to A for life, | on condition that A never sells alcohol on the property.
A: possessory estate in life estate subject to a condition subsequent

3-26 O to A from September 1, 2002, until August 31, 2008. |
A: possessory estate in a term of years

3-27 O to A for 30 years while A resides on the premises. |
A: term of years determinable

3-28 O to A for the life of B. |
A: life estate pur autre vie

3-29 O to A and the heirs of her body so long as the property is farmed, | but if the land ceases to be farmed, then back to O.
A: possessory estate in fee tail determinable

3-30 O has the right to possession because A's estate was a fee simple determinable, which ended automatically.

3-31 A has the right to possession because A's estate was a fee simple subject to a condition subsequent, which does not end automatically. O must take some action to reclaim the land.

3-32 "You can convey to your daughter a fee simple subject to a condition subsequent with the triggering event being her marriage. That way, you wouldn't have to expressly condition your right to reclaim the land on your disapproval, since that would add unnecessarily to the family tension. You can explain to her that you want her to have the house to help her get started in life, but that when she marries, presumably she and her new spouse will be able to support themselves. Ultimately, if she marries someone of whom you approve, you don't have to exercise your right to reclaim the property. You can tell your daughter at that point that you've decided to let her keep the property anyway." [*Note:* The attorney would have to take particular care in drafting this conveyance. The common law frowns on conveyances that "penalize" marriage as opposed to those that are designed to provide support until marriage, so the conveyance and its supporting documents should clarify the latter intention.]

3-33 "What Ms. Baker conveyed to the church is a fee simple determinable, which lasts only until the land is no longer used as a church. Since that triggering event (the cessation of use as a church) appears to have happened, the possessory estate had probably already returned to Ms. Baker by the time of your injury. Therefore, Ms. Baker may be liable for injuries sustained on the property, even if she didn't know that the church had closed and even if no other documents had been filed at the Courthouse." [*Note:* In some jurisdictions, statutes would cover this question and might alter the result.]

3-34 "Yes. You can do one of two things: (1) You can convey to your niece a fee simple determinable that will end automatically upon your return to live in this country. Your niece will have the rights and responsibilities of an owner, but only until you return. You will be able to reclaim the property automatically, though as a practical matter, you'll want to have your niece execute a quit claim deed or a release back to you upon your return so you can establish record title. (2) You can convey a fee simple subject to a condition subsequent. The only practical difference is that this second option doesn't operate automatically. Therefore, you could return to this country and decide at that point whether to let your niece keep the property despite your return." [*Note:* In some jurisdictions, statutes would cover this question and might alter the result.]

CHAPTER 4

4-1 None

4-2 Reversion

4-3 Reversion

4-4 Possibility of reverter

4-5 Right of entry

4-6 Reversion

4-7 Reversion

4-8 Reversion

4-9 Right of entry

4-10 Reversion and possibility of reverter

4-11 O to A so long as A does not divorce B, | then back to O.
A: possessory estate in fee simple determinable
O: possibility of reverter in fee simple absolute

4-12 O to A and her heirs so long as A does not divorce B, | but if A divorces B, then back to O.
A: possessory estate in fee simple determinable
O: possibility of reverter in fee simple absolute

4-13 O to A and his heirs, | but if A divorces B, then to O.
A: possessory estate in fee simple subject to a condition subsequent
O: right of entry in fee simple absolute

4-14 O to A, | on the condition that A does not divorce B.
A: possessory estate in fee simple subject to a condition subsequent
O: right of entry in fee simple absolute

4-15 O to A and his heirs, | provided that A does not divorce B, then to O.
A: possessory estate in fee simple subject to a condition subsequent
O: right of entry in fee simple absolute

4-16 O to A until A divorces B, | then back to O.
A: possessory estate in fee simple determinable
O: possibility of reverter in fee simple absolute

4-17 O to A; | however, if A divorces B, then to O.
A: possessory estate in fee simple subject to a condition subsequent
O: right of entry in fee simple absolute

4-18 O to A and her heirs while A refrains from divorcing B. |
A: possessory estate in fee simple determinable
O: possibility of reverter in fee simple absolute

4-19 O to A and her heirs during the time that A refrains from divorcing B, | then back to O.
A: possessory estate in fee simple determinable
O: possibility of reverter in fee simple absolute

4-20 O to A. | (Assume modern law.)
A: possessory estate in fee simple absolute
O: no interest

4-21 O to A, | provided that A never drills for oil on the property.
A: possessory estate in fee simple subject to a condition subsequent
O: right of entry in fee simple absolute

4-22 O to A and his heirs for so long as A cares for B on the premises. |
A: possessory estate in fee simple determinable
O: possibility of reverter in fee simple absolute

4-23 O to A for life or until B graduates from medical school. |
A: possessory estate in life estate determinable
O: reversion in fee simple absolute

4-24 O to A and the heirs of his body. |
A: possessory estate in fee tail

O: reversion in fee simple absolute

4-25 O to A for life, | on condition that A never sell alcohol on the property.
A: possessory estate in life estate subject to a condition subsequent
O: reversion in fee simple absolute

4-26 O to A from September 1, 2002, until August 31, 2008. |
A: possessory estate in a term of years
O: reversion in fee simple absolute

4-27 O to A for 30 years while A resides on the premises. |
A: term of years determinable
O: reversion in fee simple absolute

4-28 O to A for the life of B. |
A: life estate pur autre vie
O: reversion in fee simple absolute

4-29 O to A and the heirs of her body so long as the property is farmed, | but if the land ceases to be farmed, then back to O.
A: possessory estate in fee tail determinable
O: reversion in fee simple absolute

CHAPTER 5

5-1 Remainder

5-2 Remainder

5-3 Remainder

5-4 Remainder

5-5 Its holder is unascertained or it contains a condition precedent or both.

5-6 Its holder is ascertained and it has no condition precedent.

5-7 The person is born and identified.

5-8 A condition that (a) is set out within the description of a particular estate and (b) must be satisfied before that estate can become possessory.

5-9 Contingent remainders are "alternative" when they each follow the same estate and when their conditions precedent are the opposite of each other, so that the vesting of one precludes the vesting of the other.

5-10 Vested

5-11 Vested

5-12 Vested

5-13 The grantor

5-14 The grantee

5-15 A *remainder* is a future interest created when a grantor conveys an inherently limited possessory estate and, in the same conveyance, conveys the future interest to a second grantee. A *reversion* is a future interest created when a grantor conveys an inherently limited possessory estate and retains the future interest.

5-16 Look to see if the *next* estate is held by the grantor or a grantee. If it is held by the grantor, work above the line. If it is held by a grantee, work below the line.

5-17 (a) By deciding whether to work above or below the line in column 2 and then following the arrow or (b) by observing whether the estate column 3 describes is in a grantor or in a grantee. If it is in the grantor, work above the line; if it is in a grantee, work below the line.

5-18 O to A for life, <u>then to B.</u> (Yes)

5-19 O to A for life, <u>then to A's first child</u>. (Yes)

5-20 O to A for life, <u>then to A's heirs</u>. (No)

5-21 O to A for life, <u>then to B and her heirs</u>. (Yes)

5-22 O to A for life, <u>then to A's widow</u>. (No)

5-23 O to A for life, <u>then to A's first child</u>. (No)

5-24 O to A for life, <u>then to this year's first-year law students at State University Law School who pass the bar</u>. (No)

5-25 O to A for life, | <u>then to B if B has refrained from drinking alcoholic beverages for the 5 years prior to A's death</u>. | (Yes)

5-26 O to A for life, | <u>then to B if B has reached 21</u>. | (No)

5-27 O to A for life, | <u>then to B</u>; | however, if B ever drills for oil on the land, then to C. (No)

5-28 O to A for life, | <u>then to B,</u> | on condition that B has passed the bar. (No)

5-29 O to A for life, | <u>then to B,</u> | on condition that B has passed the bar. (Vested)

5-30 O to A for life, | <u>then to B,</u> | but if B uses the land for an insurance agency, then back to O. (Vested)

5-31 O to A for life, | <u>then to B if B does not then own an insurance agency</u>. | (Contingent)

5-32 O to A for life, | <u>then to B if B is then married</u>. | (Contingent)

5-33 O to A for life, | <u>then to B</u>; | however, if B divorces after A dies, then to O. (Vested)

5-34 O to A for life, | <u>then to A's surviving cousins</u>. | (Contingent)

5-35 O to A for life, | <u>then to A's children</u>. | (Vested)

5-36 O to A for life, | <u>then to the 2001 graduates of O's law school</u>. | (Vested)

5-37 O to A for life, | <u>then to A's widow</u>. (Contingent)

5-38 O to A for life, | <u>then to B's heirs</u>. | (Contingent)

5-39 A's heirs have a contingent remainder.

5-40 A's heirs have nothing. "And her heirs" simply identifies the nature of A's estate: a fee simple.

5-41 A has a possessory estate in life estate, and B has a vested remainder in fee simple absolute.

5-42 A has a possessory estate in life estate, and O has a reversion in fee simple absolute.

5-43 A has a possessory estate in fee simple determinable, and O has a possibility of reverter in fee simple absolute.

5-44 A has a possessory estate in fee simple subject to a condition subsequent, and O has a right of entry in fee simple absolute.

5-45 A has a possessory estate in fee simple determinable, and O has a possibility of reverter in fee simple absolute.

5-46 A has a possessory estate in fee simple subject to a condition subsequent, and O has a right of entry in fee simple absolute.

5-47 A has a possessory estate in life estate subject to a condition subsequent, and O has a reversion in fee simple absolute. [O actually has two interests: a reversion (because A's estate is a life estate) and a right of entry (because the life estate is also subject to a condition subsequent). We call O's interest the larger of these two: a reversion.]

5-48 A has a possessory estate in life estate determinable, and O has a reversion in fee simple absolute. [O actually has two interests: a reversion (because A's estate is a life estate) and a possibility of reverter (because the life estate is also determinable). We call O's interest the larger of these two: a reversion.]

5-49 O to A for life, then to B, but if B has not graduated from college, then to C. (Vested)

   O to A for life, then to B if B has graduated from college, but if not, then to C. (Contingent)

5-50 Yes

5-51 No

5-52 Yes

5-53 No

5-54 Yes

5-55 Yes

5-56 Yes

5-57 No

5-58 Vested

5-59 Contingent (A condition precedent remains: The child must survive A.)

5-60 Vested (The condition precedent was satisfied when B married.)

5-61 Contingent

CHAPTER 6

6-1 Executory interest

6-2 Executory interest

6-3 Executory interest

6-4 A grantee

6-5 An executory interest is a future interest held by a grantee, while a right of entry or possibility of reverter is a future interest retained by the grantor.

6-6 Until, while, during, so long as

6-7 But if, however, on condition that, provided that

6-8 Yes

6-9 Remainder

6-10 Right of entry

6-11 O to A and his heirs, | but if A does not graduate from college, then to B. |
A: possessory estate in fee simple subject to executory limitation
B: executory interest in fee simple absolute

6-12 O to A while being used as a farm. |
A: possessory estate in fee simple determinable
O: possibility of reverter in fee simple absolute

6-13 O to A and her heirs until no longer used for a church, | then to B.
A: possessory estate in fee simple determinable
B: executory interest in fee simple absolute

6-14 O to A for life. |
A: possessory estate in life estate
O: reversion in fee simple absolute

6-15 O to A and her heirs; | however, if used for a pool hall, then to B and his heirs. |
A: possessory estate in fee simple subject to an executory limitation
B: executory interest in fee simple absolute

6-16 O to A and her heirs, | provided that the land is always farmed. |
A: possessory estate in fee simple subject to a condition subsequent
O: right of entry in fee simple absolute

6-17 O to A, | on condition that the land is always used as a church, but if not, then to B. |
A: possessory estate in fee simple subject to an executory limitation
B: executory interest in fee simple absolute

6-18 O to A and the heirs of his body. |
A: possessory estate in fee tail
O: reversion in fee simple absolute

6-19 O to A for the life of B. |
A: possessory estate in life estate pur autre vie
O: reversion in fee simple absolute

6-20 O to A, | but if A cuts timber on the property, then to B and her heirs. |
A: possessory estate in fee simple subject to an executory limitation
B: executory interest in fee simple absolute

6-21 O to A for life; | however, if A rents the property, then to B and his heirs. |
A: possessory estate in life estate subject to an executory limitation
B: executory interest in fee simple absolute
O: reversion in fee simple absolute [O has a reversion because if A doesn't rent the property, B's future interest will never become possessory, and the property will revert to O after A's life estate.]

6-22 O to A for 25 years if A so long live. |
A: possessory estate in a term of years determinable
O: reversion in fee simple absolute

6-23 O to A for 49 years or until the land lies fallow, whichever is first, | then to B. |
A: possessory estate in a term of years determinable
B: vested remainder in fee simple absolute

6-24 O to A for life, | then to B. |
A: possessory estate in life estate
B: vested remainder in fee simple absolute

6-25 O to A and her heirs until B reaches 25, | then to B. |
A: possessory estate in fee simple determinable
B: executory interest in fee simple absolute

6-26 O to A and her heirs; | however, if B reaches 25, then to B. |

A: possessory estate in fee simple subject to an executory limitation

B: executory interest in fee simple absolute

6-27 O to A for life or until B reaches 25, | then to B. |
A: possessory estate in life estate determinable
B: vested remainder in fee simple absolute
O: no future interest [O has no reversion because B doesn't have to reach 25 in order to become possessory. The condition "until B reaches 25" is simply one way A's life estate can end. Whether A's life estate ends by A's death or by B's 25th birthday, B's future interest will become possessory. Even if B dies before A dies, B's interest will become possessory, enjoyed by B's heirs or devisees.]

6-28 O to A and her heirs, | on condition that A does not use the property for a tavern, but if A uses the property for a tavern, then to B. |
A: possessory estate in fee simple subject to an executory limitation
B: executory interest in fee simple absolute

6-29 O to A, | provided that the city does not change the property's zoning classification, otherwise to B. |
A: possessory estate in fee simple subject to an executory limitation
B: executory interest in fee simple absolute

6-30 O to A while A is attending State University, | then to B. |
A: possessory estate in fee simple determinable
B: executory interest in fee simple absolute

6-31 "Yes. You can give Christine a life estate to extend for as long as she is taking care of Timothy in the home. When she is no longer able to care for him in the home, the possessory estate would pass to all of your children, and they would be able to sell or rent the property. A life estate would give Christine sufficient control over the house so she wouldn't have to involve the rest of the family in maintenance, repairs, and routine remodeling. However, she wouldn't be able to do things that would significantly decrease the value of the property in the future. That way everyone's interests would be protected. The formal name for Christine's estate would be a possessory estate in life estate determinable (or subject to an executory limitation, depending on how we phrase it). The formal name for the future interest given to all the children together would be an executory interest in fee simple absolute."

6-32 "You can convey to the church what's called a fee simple determinable and convey to the Bibb County Library a future interest called an executory interest. You'll have to decide exactly what limitation to put on the church. For instance, do you want the possessory estate to go to the Library if the church stops using the land for worship, religious education, and fellowship, or would you still want the church to be able to 'use' the property by renting it out and collecting the proceeds? As soon as you decide precisely what limitation you want to place on the church, we can draft a conveyance that will do exactly what you wish."

6-33 "The will gave Jim a fee simple determinable and gave you an executory interest in fee simple absolute. This means that if Jim stops farming the land, even if it's for a good reason, his possessory estate automatically ends and you automatically become the owner. The way the will is worded, you have no limitation on your ownership. That means that you do not have to farm the land. A fee simple owner can sell the land, rent it, give it away, let it lie fallow, develop it, farm it, or use it in any other lawful way. If you want to sell it or keep it, using it and its proceeds entirely for yourself, you can do that. Or, if you think that your parents would have wanted you to farm the land and you're willing to farm it, you can do that. If you think they'd rather that you sell it and divide the proceeds with Jim, you can do that as well. You might want to talk to Jim about the situation before you decide."

CHAPTER 7

Assume modern law in a jurisdiction that recognizes fee tail.

7-1 A vested remainder is subject to divestment if the divesting condition could happen before the remainder becomes possessory.

7-2 A remainder is "subject to open" if it is given to a class that could expand.

7-3 A remainder given to a class is "closed" if no additional members can be added to the class.

7-4 Vested subject to divestment

7-5 Contingent

7-6 Vested and not subject to divestment

7-7 Vested subject to divestment (assuming that the condition is meant to limit A's life estate too).

7-8 Subject to open

7-9 Closed (T is dead and can have no more children.)

7-10 Closed

7-11 Subject to open

7-12 A: possessory estate in life estate
B: vested remainder in life estate
C: vested remainder in fee simple subject to a condition subsequent
O: right of entry in fee simple absolute

7-13 A: possessory estate for a term of years
B: vested remainder subject to divestment in fee simple subject to executory limitation
C: executory interest in fee simple determinable
D: executory interest in fee simple absolute

7-14 A: possessory estate in life estate
B: vested remainder in fee simple determinable
C: executory interest in fee simple subject to a condition subsequent
O: right of entry in fee simple absolute
(Some sources would say that O has a reversion following a series of contingent interests.)

7-15 A: possessory estate in life estate
B: contingent remainder in fee simple absolute
C: contingent remainder in fee simple absolute
D: contingent remainder in fee simple absolute

7-16 A: possessory estate in life estate
B: contingent remainder in life estate
C: contingent remainder in life estate pur autre vie
O: vested remainder in fee simple absolute

7-17 A: possessory estate in life estate
B: vested remainder for a term of years
X: vested remainder subject to divestment in fee simple subject to executory limitation and subject to open
D: executory interest in fee simple absolute

7-18 A: possessory estate in life estate
B: vested remainder in fee simple absolute
C: nothing
D: nothing

CHAPTER 8

Assume modern law in a jurisdiction that recognizes fee tail.

8-1 Springing executory interest

8-2 Shifting executory interest

8-3 A: possessory estate in fee simple subject to an executory limitation
B: shifting executory interest in fee simple absolute

8-4 A: possessory estate in life estate subject to an executory limitation

A's oldest child: contingent remainder in life estate subject to an executory limitation

C: shifting executory interest in fee simple absolute

O: reversion in fee simple absolute

8-5 O: possessory estate in fee simple subject to an executory limitation

A: springing executory interest in fee simple absolute

8-6 O: possessory estate in fee simple subject to an executory limitation

O's brother: springing executory interest in fee simple absolute

8-7 A: possessory estate in life estate

B: a vested remainder subject to divestment in fee simple subject to executory limitation

C: shifting executory interest in fee simple absolute

8-8 A: possessory estate in life estate

B: vested remainder in fee simple subject to an executory limitation

C: shifting executory interest in fee simple absolute

8-9 A: possessory estate in a term of years

O: reversion in fee simple subject to an executory limitation

B: springing executory interest in fee simple absolute

8-10 A: possessory estate in life estate

O: reversion in fee simple subject to an executory limitation

B: springing executory interest in fee simple absolute

8-11 A: possessory estate in life estate

O: reversion in fee simple subject to an executory limitation

C: springing executory interest in fee simple absolute

8-12 A: possessory estate in life estate

A's youngest child: contingent remainder in life estate determinable (the holder is unascertained because A might have more children.)

O: reversion in fee simple absolute

8-13 A: possessory estate in a term of years

B: vested remainder in fee simple subject to a condition subsequent

O: right of entry in fee simple absolute

8-14 A: possessory estate in life estate

O: reversion in fee simple subject to an executory limitation

B: springing executory interest in fee simple absolute

CHAPTER 9

9-1 A: possessory estate in life estate
B: vested remainder in fee simple absolute
C: nothing

9-2 A: possessory estate in life estate
B's heirs: contingent remainder in fee simple absolute
C's heirs: contingent remainder in fee simple absolute
O: reversion in fee simple absolute

9-3 A: possessory estate in fee simple determinable
O: possibility of reverter in fee simple absolute

9-4 A: possessory estate for a term of years
B: vested remainder subject to divestment in fee simple subject to executory limitation.
C: a shifting executory interest in fee simple absolute

9-5 A: possessory estate in fee simple determinable
B: shifting executory interest in fee simple absolute

9-6 A: possessory estate for a term of years
B: vested remainder in fee simple subject to an executory limitation
C: a shifting executory interest in fee simple absolute

9-7 A: possessory estate in fee simple subject to a condition subsequent
O: right of entry in fee simple absolute

9-8 O: possessory estate in fee simple subject to an executory limitation
A: springing executory interest in fee simple absolute

9-9 A: possessory estate in life estate
B: contingent remainder in fee simple absolute
C's children: contingent remainder in fee simple absolute
O: reversion in fee simple absolute

9-10 A: possessory estate in life estate
B: vested remainder subject to divestment in fee simple subject to executory limitation
C: shifting executory interest in fee simple absolute

9-11 A: possessory estate in life estate
B: contingent remainder in fee simple absolute
X: contingent remainder in fee simple absolute

9-12 C: possessory estate in life pur autre vie
B: remainder in fee simple absolute

9-13 A: possessory estate in life estate
The Dean: contingent remainder in fee simple absolute
O: reversion in fee simple absolute

9-14 A: possessory estate in life estate
B: contingent remainder in fee simple absolute
O: reversion in fee simple absolute

9-15 A: possessory estate in life estate
B: vested remainder in fee simple subject to an executory limitation
C: executory interest in fee simple absolute

9-16 A: possessory estate in life estate
O: reversion in fee simple subject to an executory limitation
B: springing executory interest in fee simple absolute

9-17 A: possessory estate in fee simple subject to an executory limitation
B: shifting executory interest in fee simple absolute

CHAPTER 11

11-1 Merger

11-2 Destruction of contingent remainders

11-3 (a) They must come into the hands of the same person.
(b) They must not be separated by another vested interest.

11-4 It ceases to exist.

11-5 Possessory estate in fee simple subject to an executory limitation

11-6 No. B's vested interest prevents merger.

11-7 Yes. C's interest is not vested.

11-8 No. The interests were created in the same document, and the two vested estates are separated by a contingent estate.

11-9 Yes. Two vested estates came into A's hands from two separate documents, and they are separated only by a contingent estate.

11-10 O to A for 10 years, then to B for life, then back to O.

A: possessory estate for a term of years
B: vested remainder in life estate
O: reversion in fee simple absolute

O subsequently conveys to C.

A: possessory estate for a term of years
B: vested remainder in life estate
C: reversion in fee simple absolute

C subsequently conveys to B.

A: possessory estate for a term of years
B: reversion in fee simple absolute

[If you did not study the doctrine of merger, simply say that B has both a vested remainder in life estate and a reversion in fee simple absolute.]

11-11 O to A for life, then to the Mayor of New York City if A has married, but if A never married, then to B. (A has not yet married.)

O: reversion in fee simple absolute
A: possessory estate in life estate
Mayor: contingent remainder in fee simple absolute
B: contingent remainder in fee simple absolute

Subsequently, A marries.

O: reversion in fee simple absolute
A: possessory estate in life estate
Mayor: vested remainder in fee simple absolute

11-12 O to A for 10 years, then to B.

A: possessory estate for a term of years
B: vested remainder in fee simple absolute

Subsequently, B dies, devising all her property to C.

A: possessory estate for a term of years
C: vested remainder in fee simple absolute

11-13 O to A for life, then to B and his heirs, but if B ever allows strip mining on the property, then to C and her heirs.

A: possessory estate in life estate
B: vested remainder in fee simple subject to an executory limitation
C: executory interest in fee simple absolute

Subsequently, B dies.

A: possessory estate in life estate
B's heirs or devisees: vested remainder in fee simple absolute
C: nothing

11-14 [*Omit if you did not study merger.*] O to A for life, then to B if B gets married. (B is unmarried.)

A: possessory estate in life estate
B: contingent remainder in fee simple absolute
O: reversion in fee simple absolute

Two years later A convey to O.

O: possessory estate in fee simple absolute

11-15 O to A for life, then to A's first child to reach 21. [A's only child (B) is 17.]

A: possessory estate in life estate
A's first child to reach 21: contingent remainder in fee simple absolute
O: reversion in fee simple absolute

Two years later A dies.

If you apply destruction of contingent remainders:
O: possessory estate in fee simple absolute

If you do not apply destruction of contingent remainders:
O: possessory estate in fee simple subject to an executory limitation
B's first child to reach 21: springing executory interest in fee simple absolute

11-16 O to A for 2 years, then to B; however, if B ever uses illegal drugs, then to C.

A: possessory estate for a term of years (assuming that B's use of drugs is meant to limit only B's remainder and not A's term of years)
B: vested remainder subject to divestment in fee simple subject to an executory limitation
C: executory interest in fee simple absolute

Two years pass.

B: possessory estate in fee simple subject to an executory limitation
C: executory interests in fee simple absolute

11-17 O (who owns in fee tail) to A. (Assume modern law.)
A: possessory estate in fee simple absolute

Then A conveys to O

O: possessory estate in fee simple absolute

11-18 O to A for life, then to B's first child and his heirs. (B has no children.)

A: possessory estate in life estate
B's first child: contingent remainder in fee simple absolute
O: reversion in fee simple absolute

Subsequently, B and her husband (C) have a child (D), who lives for one hour.

A: possessory estate in life estate
D's heirs (B and C): vested remainder in fee simple absolute

B and C have three more children (E, F, and G).

No change.

Then A, B, and C die in a car accident, all without wills.

B's and C's heirs (E, F, and G): possessory estate in fee simple absolute

11-19 O to A for life, then to B, but if B gets divorced, B's interest ends. (B is not divorced.)

A: possessory estate in life estate
B: vested remainder subject to divestment in fee simple subject to a condition subsequent (the classic example of a limitation that might divest a vested remainder is a limitation over to another grantee (an executory limitation), but it is possible for a reversionary interest to divest a remainder as well.)
O: right of entry

Two years later A conveys to O.

O: possessory estate in life estate pur autre vie
B: vested remainder subject to divestment in fee simple subject to a condition subsequent
O: right of entry
[No merger—intervening vested estate]

11-20 "No. James had a life estate, which ended when he died. Whether or not Jennifer is still living, James's life estate ended with his death, so no interest in 114 Dalmont Street is part of his estate."

11-21 "The deed to your grandfather provided that the land would revert to his grantor if your grandfather failed to farm the land. Assuming that your grandfather always farmed the land, neither the grantor nor the grantor's successors can claim it. By its terms, the condition did not apply to your mother, nor does it apply to you. You need not farm the land."

11-22 "Well, yes and no. Land held in fee tail must pass to the lineal descendants of the holder. If the line ends, the land reverts to the original grantor or passes to a different person entirely— someone set out in the original conveyance that created the fee tail years ago. However, modern law allows you to end the fee tail status by conveying the land to someone else during your lifetime. If you do, that person will not be bound by the fee tail status. He or she will have a normal (fee simple) ownership status. Since you want to keep the land during your life and then bequeath it by your will, you can convey the land to a straw person, who will immediately reconvey to you. You will then have a fee simple estate, and you can transfer the land to the city by your will. If you'd like, I can arrange for a straw person, and we can take care of the two conveyances here in my office."

11-23 [*Omit if you did not study merger.*] You and your mother do have an option. Since Keith is not yet 30, his life estate is still contingent. You and your mother can eliminate his life estate completely if one of you conveys your interest to the other. If your mother conveys her life estate to you, her interest and your interest will merge with each other, and Keith's contingent interest will be eliminated. Of course, that would be a very serious step to take, since it would no doubt have such serious repercussions on family relations and since you may well have some legitimate moral qualms about taking his interest away from him. As the owner of all interests in the property, however, you could let him live in the home so that he could have most of the benefits of his original life estate. You would simply be protecting the land, and possibly Keith as well, from some of the consequences of the addiction. You could also convey a life estate to Keith in the future if he overcomes his addiction."

CHAPTER 12

If you did not study the Rule in Shelley's Case, omit exercises 1, 2, 8, and 9.

If you did not study the doctrine of worthier title, omit exercises 3, 4, 6, 9, and 10.

12-1 O to A for life, then to A's heirs and their heirs.
A: possessory estate in fee simple absolute

12-2 O to A for life, then to B for life, then to A's heirs and their heirs.
A: possessory estate in life estate
B: vested remainder in life estate
A: vested remainder in fee simple absolute

12-3 O to A for life, then to O's heirs and their heirs.
A: possessory estate in life estate
O: reversion in fee simple absolute

12-4 O to A for life, then to B for life, then to O's heirs and their heirs.
A: possessory estate in life estate
B: vested remainder in life estate
O: reversion in fee simple absolute

12-5 O to A for life, then to A's children. (A has two children, B and C.)
A: possessory estate in life estate
B & C: vested remainder in fee simple (subject to open)

12-6 O to A for life, but if A divorces, then to O's heirs.
A: possessory estate in life estate
O: reversion in fee simple absolute

12-7 O to A for life, then to B. Then B conveys to A's heirs.
A: possessory estate in life estate
A's heirs: contingent remainder in fee simple absolute
B: reversion in fee simple absolute (because B was the grantor to A's heirs)

12-8 O to A for life, then to B for life, then to B's heirs and their heirs.
A: possessory estate in life estate
B: vested remainder in fee simple absolute

12-9 O to A for life, and 2 years later to O's heirs.
A: possessory estate in life estate
O: reversion in fee simple absolute

12-10 O to A for life, then to B. Then B conveys to O's heirs.

After first conveyance:
A: possessory estate in life estate
B: vested remainder in fee simple absolute

After second conveyance:
A: possessory estate in life estate
O's heirs: contingent remainder in fee simple absolute
B: reversion in fee simple absolute (because B is the grantor to O's heirs)

CHAPTER 13

13-1 "No interest is good unless it must vest [and close], if at all, not later than 21 years after some life in being at the creation of the interest."

13-2 Immediately at the time the conveyance is attempted

13-3 Future interests in a grantee

13-4 Contingent remainders
Vested remainders subject to open
Executory interests

13-5 Upon the death of the testator

13-6 Any person alive at the time of the conveyance

13-7 Yes, if the child is later born alive

13-8 Upon the death of D

13-9 The interest must be certain to *either* vest and close *or* fail within 21 years.

13-10 The Rule tests whether the interest *is sure to* vest and close, not whether it might.

13-11 Twenty-one years after the death of the last life in being

13-12 A person whose life can prove that the contingent interest is certain to either vest and close or fail within the permitted time period

CHAPTER 14

14-1 When the condition is not personal to someone;

When there is an identified age or time period of more than 21 years;

When a conveyance skips a generation;

When a conveyance requires that a holder survive someone who is merely described rather than named;

When an event would normally happen well within 21 years, but there is no guarantee that it will;

A "stacked" contingent interest.

14-2 O to A for life, then to A's first child to reach age 30. [A has two children: B (25) and C (28).]

According to the conveyance:
A: possessory estate in life estate
A's first child to reach 30: contingent remainder in fee simple absolute
O: reversion in fee simple absolute

Vulnerable interests:
A's first child to reach 30—invalid

State of the title after RAP:
A: possessory estate in life estate
O: reversion in fee simple absolute

14-3 O to A for life, then to A's first child to reach age 21. [A has two children: B (19) and C (18).]

According to the conveyance:
A: possessory estate in life estate
A's first child to reach 21: contingent remainder in fee simple absolute
O: reversion in fee simple absolute

Vulnerable interests:
A's first child to reach 21—valid

State of the title after RAP:
Same

14-4 O to A for life, then to B and her heirs if B reaches 25. (B is now 5.)

According to the conveyance:
A: possessory estate in life estate
B: contingent remainder in fee simple absolute
O: reversion in fee simple absolute

Vulnerable interests:
B's contingent remainder—valid

State of the title after RAP:
Same

14-5 O to A for life, then to A's first child for life, then to B's first child if he or she survives A's first child.
[At present, neither A nor B has children.]

According to the conveyance:
A: possessory estate in life estate
A's first child: contingent remainder in life estate
B's first child: contingent remainder in fee simple absolute
O: reversion in fee simple absolute

Vulnerable interests:
A's first child—valid
B's first child—invalid

State of the title after RAP:
A: possessory estate in life estate
A's first child: contingent remainder in life estate
O: reversion in fee simple absolute

14-6 O to A for life, then to A's first child if he survives A by 20 years. (A has no children yet.)

According to the conveyance:
A: possessory estate in life estate
O: reversion in fee simple subject to an executory limitation
A's first child: springing executory interest in fee simple absolute

Vulnerable interests:
A's first child—valid

State of the title after RAP:
Same

14-7 O to A for life, then to A's first grandchild and his or her heirs. (A has six children and no grandchildren.)

According to the conveyance:
A: possessory estate in life estate
A's first grandchild: contingent remainder in fee simple absolute
O: reversion in fee simple absolute

Vulnerable interests:
A's first grandchild—invalid

State of the title after RAP:
A: possessory estate in life estate
O: reversion in fee simple absolute

14-8 O devises to A for life, then to O's first grandchild and his or her heirs. (O has six children and no grandchildren.)

According to the conveyance:
A: possessory estate in life estate
O's first grandchild: contingent remainder in fee simple absolute
O's estate: reversion in fee simple absolute

Vulnerable interests:
O's first grandchild—valid

State of the title after RAP:
Same

14-9 O to A for life, then to B's first child to graduate from law school and his or her heirs. (B has two children; one of them is a first-year law student.)

According to the conveyance:
A: possessory estate in life estate
B's first child to graduate from law school: contingent remainder in fee simple absolute
O: reversion in fee simple absolute

Vulnerable interests:
B's first child to graduate from law school—invalid

State of the title after RAP:
A: possessory estate in life estate
O: reversion in fee simple absolute

14-10 O to A for life, then to the residuary beneficiary under A's will for life, then to that person's children who survive him or her.

According to the conveyance:
A: possessory estate in life estate
Residuary beneficiary: contingent remainder in life estate
Beneficiary's surviving children: contingent remainder in fee simple absolute
O: reversion in fee simple absolute

Vulnerable interests:
The residuary beneficiary—valid
The beneficiary's surviving children—invalid

State of the title after RAP:
A: possessory estate in life estate

Residuary beneficiary: contingent remainder in life estate
O: reversion in fee simple absolute

14-11 O to A for life, then to the residuary beneficiary under A's will for life, then to that person's children.

According to the conveyance:
A: possessory estate in life estate
Residuary beneficiary: contingent remainder in life estate
Beneficiary's children: contingent remainder in fee simple absolute
O: reversion in fee simple absolute

Vulnerable interests:
Residuary beneficiary—valid
Beneficiary's surviving children—invalid

State of the title after RAP:
A: possessory estate in life estate
Residuary beneficiary: contingent remainder in life estate
O: reversion in fee simple absolute

14-12 O to A and her heirs as long as the land is used for educational purposes; and if it is not used for educational purposes, then to B and her heirs.

According to the conveyance:
A: possessory estate in fee simple determinable
B: executory interest in fee simple absolute

Vulnerable interests:
B's executory interest—invalid

State of the title after RAP:
A: possessory estate in fee simple determinable
O: possibility of reverter in fee simple absolute

14-13 O devises "to the next President of the United States upon his or her swearing in."

According to the conveyance:
O's estate: possessory estate in fee simple subject to an executory limitation
Next President to be sworn in: springing executory interest in fee simple absolute

Vulnerable interests:
Next President—invalid

State of the title after RAP:
O's estate: possessory estate in fee simple absolute

14-14 O to A for life, then to B and her heirs, but if B ever sells liquor on the land, to C and her heirs.

According to the conveyance:
A: possessory estate in life estate
B: vested remainder in fee simple subject to an executory limitation
C: executory interest in fee simple absolute

Vulnerable interests:
C's executory interest—valid

State of the title after RAP:
Same

14-15 O to A for life, then to A's children and their heirs.

Assume that A has no children:
According to the conveyance:
A: possessory estate in life estate
A's children: contingent remainder in fee simple absolute
O: reversion in fee simple absolute

Vulnerable interests:
A's children—valid

State of the title after RAP:
Same

Assume that A has one child, X:
According to the conveyance:
A: possessory estate in life estate
X: vested remainder in fee simple (subject to open)

Vulnerable interests:
X's remainder—valid

State of the title after RAP:
Same

14-16 O to A for life, then to A's children who reach age 30. [A has two children: B (30) and C (28).]

According to the conveyance:
A: possessory estate in life estate
B: vested remainder in fee simple (subject to open)

Vulnerable interests:
B's remainder—invalid

State of the title after RAP:
A: possessory estate in life estate
O: reversion in fee simple absolute

14-17 See if you can solve this mystery on your own. Consult with your classmates to see if your answer matches theirs. Perhaps your professor will allow you to discuss your answer in class.

CHAPTER 15

15-1 The remainder to A's first child to join law enforcement is saved by the destructibility doctrine.

15-2 The executory interest to Habitat is void under the Rule Against Perpetuities.

15-3 The executory interest to Habitat is valid because of the charitable exemption to the Rule Against Perpetuities.

15-4 The remainder to B's grandchild is saved by the destructibility doctrine.

CHAPTER 16

If you did not study the following doctrines, omit these questions:
Rule in Shelley's Case: 8, 24, 25
Doctrine of worthier title: 13
Merger: 8, 10, 24
Destruction of contingent remainders: 11, 19, 21, 26
Rule Against Perpetuities: 4, 14, 22, 26

16-1 O to A for life, then to B and his heirs, then to C and his heirs.
A: possessory estate in life estate
B: vested remainder in fee simple absolute
C: nothing [There is nothing left to convey after A's and G's interests.]

16-2 O to A for life, then to B's heirs, then to C's heirs.
A: possessory estate in life estate
B's heirs: contingent remainder in fee simple absolute
C's heirs: contingent remainder in fee simple absolute
O: reversion in fee simple absolute

16-3 O to A and her heirs as long as the land is used for educational purposes.
A: fee simple determinable
O: possibility of reverter in fee simple absolute

16-4 O to A and her heirs as long as the land is used for educational purposes, but if the land is not used for educational purposes, then to B and his heirs.
A: fee simple determinable
[*B's executory interest is invalidated by the Rule Against Perpetuities*]
O: possibility of reverter in fee simple absolute

16-5 O to A and her heirs, but if she stops using the land for educational purposes, then to O.

A: fee simple subject to a condition subsequent
O: right of entry in fee simple absolute

16-6 O to A if she graduates from law school. (A has not yet graduated from law school.)
O: fee simple subject to an executory limitation
A: springing executory interest in fee simple absolute

16-7 O to A for life, then to B if B survives A, but if B does not survive A, to C's children. (C has one child, X.)
A: possessory estate in life estate
B: contingent remainder in fee simple absolute
X: (alternative) contingent remainder in fee simple subject to open

16-8 O to A for life, then to A's heirs.
A: possessory estate in life estate
A: vested remainder in fee simple absolute (Shelley's Case)
[*Merger combines these into a possessory estate in fee simple absolute.*]

16-9 *First conveyance:* **O to A for life, then to B and her heirs.**
Second conveyance: **A to C.**
C: life estate pur autre vie (measured by A's life)
B: vested remainder in fee simple absolute

16-10 *First conveyance:* **O to A for life, then to B if B survives A.**
Second conveyance: **O conveys to A.**
After the first conveyance:
A: possessory estate in life estate
B: contingent remainder
O: reversion.

After the second conveyance:
A: possessory estate in life estate
B: contingent remainder
A: O's reversion
Effect of merger: A's life estate merges into the reversion, destroying B's contingent remainder. Therefore, A has a possessory estate in fee simple absolute.

16-11 O to A for life, then to B if B marries. (B is unmarried.) A dies and B is still unmarried.

According to the conveyance:
A: possessory estate in life estate
B: contingent remainder in fee simple absolute
O: reversion

Upon A's death:
The doctrine of destructibility of contingent remainders destroys

B's contingent remainder. O has a possessory estate in fee simple absolute.

16-12 O to A for life, then to B if B adopts A's surviving children.
A: possessory estate in life estate
O: reversion in fee simple subject to an executory limitation
B: springing executory interest in fee simple absolute

16-13 O to A for life, then to O's heirs.
A: possessory estate in life estate
O: reversion in fee simple absolute [worthier title]

16-14 O to A for life, then to A's widow for life, then to A's children who survive A's widow. [A is now married and has a child (B).]
A: possessory estate in life estate
A's widow: contingent remainder in life estate
[*B's contingent remainder in fee simple absolute is invalidated by the Rule Against Perpetuities*]
O: reversion in fee simple absolute

16-15 *First conveyance:* **O to A for life.**
Second conveyance: **O to B and C.**
After the second conveyance:
A: possessory estate in life estate
B and C: O's reversion in fee simple absolute

16-16 O to A for life, then to A's children. (A has one child, B.)
A: possessory estate in life estate
B: vested remainder in fee simple subject to open
[Shelley's Case doesn't apply to "A's children," only to "A's heirs."]

16-17 *First conveyance:* **O to A for life, then to B, but if B sells liquor on the premises, to O.**
Second conveyance: **A inherits from O.**

After the first conveyance:
A: possessory estate in life estate
B: vested remainder in fee simple subject to a condition subsequent
O: right of entry in fee simple absolute

After the second conveyance:
A: life estate
B: vested remainder in fee simple subject to a condition subsequent
A: O's right of entry
[*The intervening vested remainder prevents merger.*]

16-18 *First conveyance:* **O to A for life, then to B.**
Second conveyance: **B conveys to O's heirs.**

After the first conveyance:
A: possessory estate in life estate
B: vested remainder in fee simple absolute.

After the second conveyance:
A: possessory estate in life estate
O's heirs: contingent remainder in fee simple absolute
B (as the grantor in the second conveyance): reversion in fee simple absolute
[*Merger doesn't apply because the interests are created in two instruments.*]

16-19 O to A for life, then to B's heirs, and if B has no heirs, then to C. (Then A dies and B is still alive.)

According to the conveyance:
A: possessory estate in life estate
B's heirs: contingent remainder in fee simple absolute
C: contingent remainder in fee simple absolute
O: reversion in fee simple absolute

When A dies and B is still alive:
O: possessory estate in fee simple absolute.
[The contingent remainder to B's heirs is destroyed by the doctrine of destruction of contingent remainders.]
[The contingent remainder to C suffers the same fate (assuming a court would construe "if B has no heirs" as a condition precedent and not yet satisfied, and therefore would destroy C's interest, too).]

16-20 O to A for life, then to B's heirs, and if B has no heirs, then to C. (Then B dies with heirs. Then A dies.)

According to the conveyance:
A: possessory estate in life estate
B's heirs: contingent remainder
C: contingent remainder
O: reversion in fee simple absolute

After B dies with heirs:
B's heirs: vested remainder in fee simple absolute
[C's contingent remainder is destroyed by the vesting of B's heirs' remainder.]

After A dies:
B's heirs: possessory estate in fee simple absolute

16-21 O to A for life, then to B if B graduates from law school, but if B does not graduate from law school, then to C. (Then A dies. B is two weeks away from graduating from law school.)

At the time of the conveyance:
A: possessory estate in life estate

B: contingent remainder in fee simple absolute
C: contingent remainder in fee simple absolute
O: reversion in fee simple absolute

When A dies, the doctrine of destruction of contingent remainders operates:
[B's remainder is still contingent on graduation, so it is destroyed.]
[C's remainder is still contingent on B not graduating, but B is still alive and still might graduate. So C's remainder is destroyed, too.]
Therefore, O: possessory estate in fee simple absolute.

16-22 O to A for life, then to B's first child to become a doctor. (B has two children, ages 2 and 5.)
A: possessory estate in life estate
[B's first child to become a doctor: contingent remainder, which is invalidated by the Rule Against Perpetuities]
O: reversion in fee simple absolute

16-23 O devises to A for life, then to A's first grandchild. (A has three children and two grandchildren.)
A: possessory estate in life estate
A's first grandchild: vested remainder in fee simple absolute
[A's first grandchild is a life in being and is already vested.]

16-24 O to A for life, then to A's heirs.

According to the conveyance:
A: possessory estate in life estate
A's heirs: contingent remainder (in fee simple absolute)
O: reversion in fee simple absolute

Applying the Rule in Shelley's Case:
A: possessory estate in life estate
A: vested remainder in fee simple absolute
[It was a contingent remainder but now the holder is ascertained.]
[O has nothing now that the remainder is vested.]

Applying merger:
A: possessory estate in fee simple absolute

16-25 O to A for life, then to B for life, then to A's heirs.

According to the conveyance:
A: possessory estate in life estate
B: vested remainder in life estate
A's heirs: contingent remainder in FSA
(because not ascertained)
O: reversion in fee simple absolute

Apply the Rule in Shelley's Case:
A: possessory estate in life estate

B: vested remainder in life estate

A: vested remainder in fee simple absolute

[It was a contingent remainder but now the holder is ascertained.]

Apply merger? No, because there is an intervening vested estate.

16-26 O to A for life, then to A's first child to reach 25. (A has no children.)

According to the conveyance:

A: life estate

A's first child to reach 25: contingent remainder

O: reversion

Applying the Rule Against Perpetuities (with destructibility), the contingent remainder will be destroyed on A's death. Therefore, the contingent remainder is valid under the RAP because it will either vest or be destroyed on A's death.

16-27 The order is:

1. Rule in Shelley's Case (and merger)
2. doctrine of worthier title (and merger)
3. Rule Against Perpetuities
4. merger
5. destruction of contingent remainders

16-28 Rule in Shelly's Case (and merger)

doctrine of worthier title (and merger)

Rule Against Perpetuities

16-29 merger

doctrine of destruction of contingent remainders

Practice Exercises for Use in Class

The following exercises are designed for use in class. Therefore, the answers are not provided in this book. Your professor's copy of the Teacher's Manual provides both the suggested answers and a list of the doctrines used in each question. That list will make it easy for your professor to identify which exercises to use in class for each estate, future interest, and doctrine covered in this book.

The exercises for each set of chapters include some questions covering material from prior chapters so you can practice distinguishing the new concepts from prior concepts.

Even if your professor does not use these exercises in class, you may wish to practice with them. Most of the exercises use names and are phrased differently from the standard "O to A" format. That different phrasing can be confusing at first, but since real-life conveyances are not phrased in the "O to A" format, it is good to get used to working with more normal language.

REVIEW EXERCISES FOR CHAPTERS 2–4: FUTURE INTERESTS IN THE GRANTOR

Give the state of the title.

1. Michael conveys the house on Adams Street to Jane and her heirs, provided that Jane is never disbarred.

2. I, Harold, devise my family home to my wife, Maude, but if she ceases to use it as her residence, her estate ends.

3. Marilyn conveys to Arthur and his heirs for so long as the land is farmed.

4. Dan conveys to Carol for her lifetime.

5. I, Carolyn, bequeath all of my real property to my husband, John; however, if John ever lives in sin with a woman, then my property will go back to my estate.

6. I grant Venita possession of 1428 Elm Street for 10 years.

7. Jay conveys to Ellen and the heirs of her body.

8. The Red Cross conveys to First City Bank until such time as the 14th Street Exit off I-75 is completed.

9. I, Joan, give my vacation home in the Catskills to my brother, James, for his life.

10. Carson Cohen conveys 101 Martin Luther King Boulevard to Apex Exterminating for 30 years.

11. I want the Simpson farm to remain in my family for as long as possible. Since I have no children, I devise the farm to my sister Janice and the heirs of her body.

12. I, John Miller Kendell, devise the real property located at 842 Avenue of the Americas to my beloved daughter Christine and her son Giles.

REVIEW EXERCISES FOR CHAPTERS 5–6: FUTURE INTERESTS IN A GRANTEE

What is the state of the title?

1. Uncle Jesse conveys to Maria for her use during her life.

2. I hereby grant and convey all my right, title, and interest in 1201 Hemlock Street to my son Charles and his heirs for as long as the property is not used for commercial purposes.

3. I, Justin Perotta, do hereby lease Apartment 2-B, Garden Arbour Apartments, to Amanda Dowlen for 5 years, and thereafter to Amanda's first child, Christopher.

4. Amanya devises all her real estate to Aaron while Aaron continues to participate actively in Doctors Without Borders, but if Aaron ceases to participate in Doctors Without Borders, then all of the property shall go to Denise and her heirs.

5. Temple Beth Israel conveys the premises at First and Main to The City Food Bank for 15 years, and thereafter the property shall revert to Temple Beth Israel.

6. I, Eleon Caraba, being of sound mind and under no duress, hereby devise my home to my son and his heirs forever. (Eleon is still alive.)

7. I grant my real property in Newtown to Pauline, on the condition that Pauline never ceases to use the property for her primary residence. All the rest of any interest in the property I grant to my son, Thomas. (Signed: Lawrence Olson)

8. I devise whatever property I am using as my law office at my death to my law partner, Kate, for her life and thereafter to my children.

9. Jennifer grants to First Congregational Church the property to the west of the present Church building, provided that the Church must always use the property for a school.

10. I, Carlotta Perez, do hereby bequeath my beach house to my daughter Juanita while Juanita has a child under the age of eighteen. When Juanita's youngest child reaches eighteen, then the property shall go to the joint ownership of all of my children and their heirs.

11. Latanya conveys all her right, title, and interest in her house to her brother Lionel.

12. The City of Newtown grants all its interest in the old train station to the Metro Transit Board, on condition that the property must be used for transportation purposes. If the property should cease to be used for transportation purposes, then the property shall pass to Ada County.

REVIEW EXERCISES FOR CHAPTERS 7–9: SHIFTING AND SPRINGING EXECUTORY INTERESTS AND REVIEW OF FUTURE INTERESTS IN A GRANTEE

What is the state of the title?

1. Alice conveys to Dennis and Kimberly, but if they should divorce, then the property shall go to Anita.

2. John Barton Carlisle hereby grants to John Philip Carlisle all his ownership interest in 447 Hill Terrace upon the day that John Philip Carlisle is sworn in to the Bar.

3. Ben conveys to Alison and her heirs, provided, however, that if Alison fails to pass the Bar examination on her first try, then to Nate.

4. Ben conveys to Alison and her heirs for as long as Alison has not failed a Bar examination.

5. Laura conveys to Gunther for his lifetime the warehouse on Tenth Street. Then one year after Gunther's death, the property shall pass to Gunther's surviving children.

6. Maizie grants to Jeff for 15 years and thereafter to Laura.

7. I, Deryl Gere, hereby grant and convey all my interest in my property at 8670 Coleman Avenue to Richard Alayansa, but if he should ever use the property to sell or store cigarette products, then the property shall pass to Sidney Jones.

8. I, Virginia Belson, hereinafter known as the Party of the First Part, do convey the premises located at 10 Knoll Road to my daughter Katherine, hereinafter known as the Party of the Second Part, on condition that she never marries Lance Harrison.

9. Carol grants all her real property to Bernadette, but if Bernadette fails to graduate from law school within 15 years, then to Alan.

CLASSROOM EXERCISES FOR CHAPTER 11: POST-CONVEYANCE DEVELOPMENTS

What is the state of the title after all of the events have occurred?

1. Maude conveys to Harold; however, if Charlie ever recants his belief in predestation, then to Charlie. (Eight years later Charlie dies without having recanted.)

2. Maude conveys to Harold for life, then to Charlie for life, then to Charlie's children. (The next day Charlie dies, leaving one child, Mary.)

3. Maude conveys to Harold for life, then to Charlie. (A year later Charlie conveys his interest back to Maude.)

4. Maude conveys to Harold for life, then to Charlie if Charlie has recanted his belief in predestination by then. Otherwise, to Lizette. (Immediately upon learning of the conveyance, Charlie recants.)

5. Maude conveys to Harold for life, then to Charlie if Charlie recants his belief in predestination before he reaches the age of 50. (Six months later Harold dies. Charlie is 30 and has not yet recanted.)

6. Maude conveys to Harold for life, then to Charlie for life if Charlie has recanted his belief in predestination, then to Lizette. (Two years later Harold has a fight with Charlie and conveys his life estate to Lizette.)

7. Maude conveys to Harold for life, then to Charlie for life; however, if Charlie has not recanted his belief in predestination by the time Harold dies, then to Lizette. (Charlie recants immediately upon learning that Harold is feeling ill.)

PRACTICE EXERCISES FOR USE IN CLASS

8. Maude conveys to Harold for life, then to Charlie for life; however, if Charlie has not recanted his belief in predestination by the time Harold dies, then to Lizette. (The next week Lizette dies.)

9. Maude conveys to Harold for life. (A year later Maude executes a quit claim deed conveying to Charlie any remaining interest she has.)

10. Maude conveys to Harold, but if Harold ever professes a belief in predestination, then to Lizette. (Subsequently, Harold dies without having professed a belief in predestination.)

11. Maude conveys to Harold for life. (Subsequently, Harold conveys to Charlie.)

12. Maude conveys to Harold for life, then to Charlie for life if Charlie has recanted his belief in predestination before Harold dies, then to Lizette. (One year later Charlie recants. Six months later Harold has a fight with Charlie and conveys his life estate to Lizette.)

CLASSROOM EXERCISES FOR CHAPTER 12

State the title, applying the doctrines covered in Chapter 12.

1. Ike to Mamie for life, then to Ike's heirs.

2. Ike to Mamie for life, then to Mamie's heirs.

3. Ike conveys to Mamie for life, then to Albert for life, then to Mamie's heirs.

4. Ike conveys to Mamie for life. (The next day Ike conveys his reversion "to my heirs.")

5. Ike conveys to Mamie for life, then to Ike's children.

6. Ike conveys to Mamie for life, then to Mamie's issue.

7. Ike conveys to Mamie for life, then to Albert for life if Albert survives Mamie, then to Ike's heirs.

8. Ike to Mamie for life, then to Albert for life if Albert is then married, then to Mamie's heirs. (Albert is now married.)

CLASSROOM EXERCISES FOR CHAPTERS 13–14: RULE AGAINST PERPETUITIES

State whether any interest in the following conveyances violates the original version of the Rule Against Perpetuities. If an interest offends the Rule, give the state of the title after the offending interest is struck.

1. O to A for 10 years, then to B, but if B ever mines the land, then to C.

2. O to A for life, then to A's youngest child for life, then to A's other children who are still alive. (At the time of the conveyance, A has three children.)

3. O to A for 10 years, then to A's first child for 10 years, then to B's oldest surviving child. (At the time of the conveyance, A and B each have one child.)

4. O to A for life, then to B for life, then to B's surviving children. (B has no children.)

5. O to A and his heirs until the land is used for commercial purposes, then to B.

6. O to A and his heirs, but if the land is used for commercial purposes, then to B.

7. O to A and her heirs as long as the land is not used for commercial purposes.

8. O to A, but if the land is used for commercial purposes within 20 years of the conveyance, then to B.

9. Testator devises to A effective upon the reading of the will.

10. O to A for life, then to A's first child for life, then to O's grandchildren in joint ownership. (A has no children. O has 2 grandchildren.)

11. O to A as long as the land is always farmed.

Collection of Outlines and Summary Boxes

OUTLINE VERSION OF CHART FOR ANALYZING CONVEYANCES

I. POSSESSORY ESTATE

Durational Nature:

1. **Fee simple** (*O to A <u>and her heirs</u>*)—unlimited duration

2. **Fee tail** (*O to A <u>and the heirs of her body</u>*)—until the line runs out

3. **Life estate** (*O to A <u>for life</u>*)—until the measuring life dies

4. **Term of years** (*O to A <u>for 10 years</u>*)—until the term expires

Added Limitation (if any):

If the estate conveyed is a fee simple with no added limitations:
1. **Absolute**

If the next interest is retained by the grantor:
2. **xxxx**
   (*the possessory estate is a fee tail, life estate, or term of years and the grantor did not add any limitations*)
3. **Determinable**
   (*the limitation uses words like "until," "during," "so long as," "while" and is placed before the punctuation mark*)
4. **Subject to a condition subsequent**
   (*the limitation uses words like "but if," "however," "on condition that," "provided that" and is placed after the punctuation mark*)

If next interest is in a grantee:
5. **xxxx**
   (*the possessory estate is a fee tail, life estate, or term of years and the grantor did not add any limitations*)
6. **Determinable**
   (*the limitation uses words like "until," "during," "so long as," "while" and is placed before the punctuation mark*)
7. **Subject to an executory limitation**
   (*the limitation uses words like "but if," "however," "on condition that," "provided that" and is placed after the punctuation mark*)

II. FUTURE INTEREST

Kind of Future Interest:

In grantor:
1. **Reversion** (*waits patiently—follows xxxx*)
2. **Possibility of reverter** (*waits patiently—follows determinable*)
3. **Right of entry** (*interrupts—follows subject to a condition subsequent*)

In grantee:
4. **Remainder** (*waits patiently—follows xxxx*)
   · vested (*ascertained taker and no condition precedent*)
   · vested subject to divestment (might be divested before becoming possessory)
   · contingent (*unascertained taker or condition precedent*)
5. **Executory interest** (*follows determinable or subject to an executory limitation*)
   · shifting (*follows estate in grantee*)
   · springing (*divests estate in grantor*)

Durational Nature:

1. **Fee simple** (*O to A <u>and her heirs</u>*)—unlimited duration
2. **Fee tail** (*O to A <u>and the heirs of her body</u>*)—until the line runs out
3. **Life estate** (*O to A <u>for life</u>*)—until the measuring life dies
4. **Term of years** (*O to A <u>for 10 years</u>*)—until the term expires

Added Limitation (if any):

If the estate conveyed is a fee simple with no added limitations:
1. **Absolute**

If the next interest is retained by the grantor:

 2. xxxx

  (the possessory estate is a fee tail, life estate, or term of years and the grantor did not add any limitations)

 3. Determinable

  (the limitation uses words like "until," "during," "so long as," "while" and is placed before the punctuation mark)

 4. Subject to a condition subsequent

  (the limitation uses words like "but if," "however," "on condition that," "provided that" and is placed after the punctuation mark)

If next interest is in a grantee:

 5. xxxx

  (the possessory estate is a fee tail, life estate, or term of years and the grantor did not add any limitations)

 6. Determinable

  (the limitation uses words like "until," "during," "so long as," "while" and is placed before the punctuation mark)

 7. Subject to an executory limitation

  (the limitation uses words like "but if," "however," "on condition that," "provided that" and is placed after the punctuation mark)

DISTINGUISHING ADDED LIMITATIONS

Determinable Estate

1. The limitation is phrased expressly as the measure of the duration of the estate, using words like *until, so long as, while,* and *during.*

2. The limitation is placed *before* the punctuation mark signaling the end of the description of A's estate.

Estate Subject to a Condition Subsequent

1. The limitation is phrased like an afterthought or a condition that allows the grantor to cut short an estate previously granted. It uses words like *but if, provided that, on condition that,* and *however.*

2. The limitation is placed *after* the punctuation mark signaling the end of the description of A's estate.

Determinable estate ends automatically.	Estate subject to condition subsequent ends only if and when 0 enforces the right to retake possession.

Possessory Estate	Grantor's Future Interest
A fee simple absolute	None
A fee tail, life estate, or term of years *(whether or not it has an added limitation)*	Reversion
A fee simple determinable *(until, during, while, as long as)*	Possibility of reverter
A fee simple subject to a condition subsequent *(but if, provided that, on condition that, however)*	Right of entry

Distinguishing Remainders and Reversions

Remainder

O to A for life, __then to B__.

Reversion

O to A for life, __then to O__.

Remainder and Reversion

Remainder
A future interest created when a grantor conveys an inherently limited possessory estate and, in the same conveyance, conveys the future interest to a second grantee.

Reversion
A future interest created when a grantor conveys an inherently limited possessory estate and retains the future interest rather than conveying it to a second grantee.

Vested and Contingent Remainders

Vested
A remainder is vested if:

1. It is given to an *ascertained* person *and*

2. It is *not subject to a condition precedent* other than the natural termination of the preceding estate.

Contingent
Conversely, a remainder is contingent if:

1. It is given to an *unascertained* person *or*

2. It is subject to a *condition precedent* other than the natural termination of the preceding estate.

Two Requirements for an Ascertained Taker

- Born
- Identified

Condition Precedent

A condition that

▶ Is set out within the description of a particular estate and

▶ Must be satisfied before that estate can become possessory.

Alternative Contingent Remainders

Contingent remainders are "alternative" when they each follow the same estate and when their conditions precedent are the opposite of each other, so that the vesting of one precludes the vesting of the other.

Identifying Contingent Remainders, Vested Remainders, and Vested Remainders Subject to Divestment

1. Draw lines separating the descriptions of the various estates.

2. Underline the remainder you're interested in.

3. Look in the underlined words for a condition precedent. If there is a condition precedent in the underlined words, the remainder is contingent. If there is no condition precedent there, the remainder is vested.[25]

4. If the remainder is vested, you have one more step to take. Look at the *next* estate. If you find a limitation that *could* divest the remainder *before it becomes possessory,* then add the term "subject to divestment" to the term "vested remainder."

Review: Remainders and Executory Interests

Vested remainder:

> *O to A for life, <u>then to B and her heirs</u>.*

Vested remainder followed by another vested remainder:

> *O to A for life, <u>then to B for life,</u>*
> <u>*then to C and her heirs*</u>.

Vested remainder (subject to divestment) (column 3) in fee simple (column 4) subject to an executory limitation (column 5):

> *O to A for life, <u>then to B,</u> but if B*
> *is not then living, to C.*

Another vested remainder subject to divestment (column 3) in fee simple (column 4) subject to an executory limitation (column 5):

> *O to A for life, <u>then to B,</u> but if B divorces, then to C.*

Contingent remainder:

> *O to A for life, <u>then to B if B is then living</u>.*

Contingent remainder followed by an alternative contingent remainder:

> *O to A for life, <u>then to B if B is then living, but if B is not then living, then to C</u>.*

[25] Assuming it is given to an ascertained taker.

NAMING AN INTEREST

Kind of Interest	Nature of Interest	Added Limitation
1. Possessory estate	1. Fee simple	1. Absolute/no limitation
2. Reversion	2. Fee tail	2. Determinable
3. Possibility of reverter	3. Life estate	3. Subject to a condition subsequent
4. Right of entry	4. Life estate pur autre vie	4. Subject to an executory limitation
5. Vested remainder	5. Term of years	5. Subject to open
6. Vested remainder subject to divestment		
7. Contingent remainder		
8. Shifting executory interest		
9. Springing executory interest		

Merger

If

1. A possessory or vested life estate and the next vested estate in fee simple come into the hands of the same person and

2. These two estates are not separated by another *vested* estate,

Then

3. The life estate merges into the next vested estate held by the same person, and

4. If there is a *contingent* remainder between them, the contingent remainder will be destroyed.
   (*Exception*: If the estates were created in the same document an intervening contingent estate is safe.)

Rule in Shelley's Case

If

1. The same document

2. Conveys a life estate to a grantee and

3. A remainder to *that grantee's* heirs,

Then

4. The conveyance to the grantee's heirs immediately becomes conveyance to the grantee.

Doctrine of Destruction of Contingent Remainders

A contingent remainder is destroyed if it is still contingent when the prior estate ends.

Doctrine of Worthier Title

If

1. The same intervivos conveyance

2. Conveys an inherently limited estate to a *grantee* and

3. A remainder or an executory interest to *the grantor's* heirs,

Then

The conveyance to the grantor's heirs is read as a conveyance to the grantor.

Rule in Shelley's Case and Merger

1. *O to A for life, then to A's heirs.*

The Rule in Shelley's Case reads the contingent remainder in A's heirs as a remainder in A.

Is the remainder still contingent? No, because now the holder of the remainder is ascertained, so the remainder is vested.

Does merger apply? Yes, because the remainder is now vested. The merger doctrine merges the life estate into the vested remainder.

2. *O to A for life, remainder to A's heirs if A survives B.*

The Rule in Shelley's Case converts the contingent remainder in A's heirs into a remainder in A.

Is the remainder in A still contingent? Yes. The holder is now ascertained, but the condition precedent remains.

Does merger apply? No, because the remainder is contingent.

3. *O to A for life, then to B for life, then to A's heirs.*

The Rule in Shelley's Case converts the contingent remainder in A's heirs into a remainder in A.

Is the remainder in A still contingent? No. Now, the holder of the remainder is ascertained. The remainder is now vested.

Does merger apply? No, because there is an intervening vested estate (B's life estate).

Review

Rule in Shelley's Case

> *O to A for life, then to ~~A's heirs~~ A.*

1. The same intervivos conveyance
2. Conveys an inherently limited estate to a grantee and
3. A remainder to *that grantee's* heirs

Doctrine of Worthier Title

> *O to A for life, then to ~~O's heirs~~ O.*

1. The same document
2. Conveys an inherently limited estate to a grantee and
3. A remainder or an executory interest to *the grantor's* heirs

Destructibility of Contingent Remainders (from Chapter 11)

> *O to A for life, ~~then to B if B is 21~~.*
>
> [A dies before B reaches 21.]

A remainder is destroyed if it does not vest at or before the termination of the preceding estate. The doctrine does not apply to executory interests.

Merger

> *O to A for life, then to B.*
>
> [Then A conveys to B.] B now has a possessory estate in the fee simple.

If

1. A possessory or vested life estate and the next vested estate in fee simple come into the hands of the same person and
2. These two estates are not separated by another *vested* estate,

Then

3. The estates merge, and
4. Any *contingent* remainder between them is destroyed.

(*Exception*: If the estates were created in the same document, an intervening contingent estate is safe.)

Contingent Interest

1. The identity of the holder is unascertained, or

2. The interest is subject to a condition precedent (other than the termination of the prior estate).

Vested Interest

1. The holder is ascertained, and

2. The interest is *not* subject to a condition precedent (other than the termination of the prior estate).

The Three Vulnerable Future Interests

Contingent remainders

Vested remainders subject to open

Executory interests

Rule Against Perpetuities

A future interest is void *the moment it's created* if

1. It is in a *grantee* (a remainder or an executory interest);

2. It is either *contingent* (given to an unascertained taker or subject to a condition precedent or both) or *subject to open*; and

3. It might still exist and *still be contingent or subject to open* longer than 21 years after the death of the last person alive at the time of the conveyance.

A Step-by-Step Approach for Applying the Rule

Step 1: Draw vertical lines to separate the different interests. Then identify the state of the title according to the conveyance.

Step 2: Look for any future interests in a *grantee*.

Step 3: If you find any future interests in a grantee, check each one to see if it is contingent or open. If so, it's vulnerable. Underline it.

Step 4: Identify the necessary factual developments for vesting and closing, and write them beside the conveyance.

Step 5: Circle all of the lives in being.

Step 6: See if the interest might *still* be contingent or open longer than the lifetimes of everyone you circled plus 21 years. Look for a validating life.

Step 7: If the contingent interest violates the Rule, strike the whole interest, and revise your classification of the title.

Step 8: If there is *another* contingent or open interest in a grantee, repeat this procedure.

RAP Danger Signs

1. The condition is not personal to someone.

2. There is an identified age or time period of more than 21 years.

3. An interest is given to a generation after the next generation (for example, to grandchildren).

4. A conveyance requires that a holder survive someone who is merely described rather than named.

5. An identified event that would normally happen well within 21 years, but might not.

6. The holder won't be identified until the death of someone merely described rather than named.

Recap of Doctrines Affecting Conveyances

The Rule in Shelley's Case

> *O to A for life, then to ~~A's heirs~~ <u>A</u>.*

The Doctrine of Worthier Title

> *O to A for life, then to ~~O's heirs~~ <u>O</u>.*

Merger
When a life estate and the next vested estate come into the hands of the same person, they are combined. If they are separated by a contingent remainder, the remainder is destroyed.

Destruction of Contingent Remainders
A remainder that is still contingent at the end of the prior estate will be destroyed.

The Rule Against Perpetuities
No interest is good unless it must either fail or vest and close within 21 years of the death of a life in being.

Applying Multiple Doctrines

At the Time of the Conveyance
1. Apply the Rule in Shelley's Case (and merger, if applicable) to any offending grantee interest.

2. Apply the doctrine of worthier title (and merger, if applicable) to any offending interest given to the grantor's heirs.

3. Apply the Rule Against Perpetuities to any vulnerable contingent or open grantee interest (keeping in mind that a contingent remainder might be saved if the jurisdiction applies the doctrine of destruction of contingent remainders).

After Subsequent Factual Developments
4. Apply merger to any vested interests that come into the hands of the same person and are not separated by another vested estate.

5. Apply the doctrine of destruction of contingent remainders to any remainder still contingent at the close of the prior estate.

INDEX

Absolute, 21-23, 31, 39-41, 46

Alternative contingent remainders, 64-65

Ancestors, 4

Battle of Hastings, 1

Bequeath, 4

Adverse possession, 30-31

Ascertained, 57-59

Assignable, 14

Bequest, 4

Charitable exemption, 166-167

Class gifts, 58

Closed interests. *See* subject to open

Collaterals, 4

Condition precedent, 56-57, 59-61,

Condition subsequent. *See* subject to condition subsequent

Contingent, 55-62, 92, 113-115, 118-122, 135-137, 141-143, 156-157

Convey, 4

Conveyance, 4

Decedent, 4

Defeasible estate, 23

Destruction of contingent remainders, 120-122, 165-166, 169-170

Determinable, 23, 25 -27, 29, 31, 34, 42, 46, 71-75, 157-158

Devise, 4

Devisee, 4

Disentail, 116

Doctrine of worthier title, 130-133, 169-170

Escheat, 4

Executory interest, 71-79, 95-99, 102-104, 113-115, 137, 157-160,

Express condition, 28

Fee simple, 9-10

Fee simple absolute. *See* absolute

Fee tail, 10 -11, 115-116,

Fertile octogenarian, 137

Fetus rule, 137

Future interest, 7

Gestation rule. *See* fetus rule

Grantee, 2

Grantor, 2

Heirs, 4
Heirs apparent, 4

Inherit, 4, 11-12
Inherently limited estate, 9-17
Inter vivos, 131
Intestate, 4
Issue, 4, 10

Life estate, 12
Life estate *pur autre vie*, 15
Life in being, 141
Lineal descendants, 4

Merger, 118-120, 129-130, 132-133, 169-170

Open interests. *See* subject to open

Possessory estate, 7
Possibility of reverter, 42 - 44, 46
Pur autre vie, 15-16

Reformation of conveyance, 167
Remainder, 51-55, 101-104, 116-117,
Reversion, 41-42, 46, 52, 55, 62-64, 116-117
Right of entry, 44 - 46
Rule Against Perpetuities, 135, 138-14, 150-160, 165-168, 169-170
Rule in Shelley's Case, 128-130, 169-170

Seisin, 13

Shelley's Case. *See* Rule in Shelley's Case
Shifting executory interest, 95-99
Springing executory interest, 95-99
Subject to a condition subsequent, 23, 27-34, 44-46
Subject to divestment. *See* vested subject to divestment
Subject to executory limitation, 75-79, 159-160,
Subject to open, 92-93, 136-138, 155-156
Subject to partial divestment, 93
Successor in interest, 2

Temporal limitation, 25
Term of years, 13-14
Testate, 4
Testator, 2

Unascertained. *See* ascertained
Unborn widow, 138

Validating life, 143-146,
Vested, 55-62, 92, 115, 118-120, 135-136, 155-160,
Vested subject to divestment, 89-92, 102-104,

Wait and see approach, 167-168
William of Normandy, 1
Words of express condition. *See* express condition
Words of limitation, 9-17
Words of purchase, 9 - 17
Words of temporal limitation. *See* temporal limitation
Worthier title. *See* Doctrine of worthier title

▶ How to Use the Chart

1. **Column 1:** Select the estate of whoever has the possessory estate.

2. **Column 2:**

   ▲ If column 1 was a fee simple and there is no added limitation, select "absolute" and stop.

   ▲ Is the next future interest held by the grantor or by a grantee?
      ▲ If by the grantor, stay above the center line.
      ▲ If by a grantee, stay below the center line.

   ▲ Does the future interest follow a fee tail, life estate, or term of years?
      ▲ If so, select the "xxxx" entry.
      ▲ If not, select from the following two descriptions:

   ▲ Is the condition limiting the column 1 estate placed within the description of the column 1 estate & does it use words like *until, during, while, as long as?* If so, select the "determinable" entry.

   ▲ Is the condition limiting the column 1 estate placed within the description of the *next* interest & does it use words like *however, on condition that, provided that, but if?* If so, select the "subject to . . ." entry.

3. **Column 3:** Simply follow the arrow from the column 2 entry to the correct column 3 entry.

4. **Column 4–9:** Start over, following these same directions for each succeeding interest.